**Fishing for Solutions**

Michael De Alessi

Published by the IEA Environment Unit, 1998

First published in February 1998 by
The Environment Unit
The Institute of Economic Affairs
2 Lord North Street
Westminster
London SW1P 3LB

IEA Studies on the Environment No. 11
ISBN 0-255 36444-X

Printed in Great Britain by
Hartington Fine Arts Limited, Lancing, West Sussex
Set in Times New Roman and Univers

Contents

Foreword

More than 70 per cent of the earth's surface is covered in water. According to the United Nations, the oceans contain around 80 per cent of the world's life forms.[1] From this vast reserve, fishermen take over 100 million tonnes of fish per year, providing a livelihood for around 200 million people.[2] But however enormous the oceans may seem, they are not infinite and, as the cod fishermen of Canada recently discovered, stocks can be depleted.

Early reports suggest that when settlers first arrived in Newfoundland in the 15th century, fish were so plentiful that they could be caught simply by lowering a bucket over the side of a boat. But by 1993, stocks had fallen so low that the Canadian Government called a unilateral moratorium on catching cod, in order to allow stocks to recover, with the consequent loss of between 15,000 and 30,000 jobs. Other fish were also affected, especially turbot, which was the subject of a 'fish war' in 1995 when a Spanish trawler, the Estai, came too close to Canada's waters, leading the Canadian government to send in the Navy.

The immediate cause of the collapse of these and other fish stocks is excessive levels of fishing. But not all cod stocks are under threat and, according to the UN Food and Agriculture Organisation, only a small proportion of the world's fish stocks are over-fished,[3] which begs the question as to why some species are over-fished in some areas, whilst in other areas the same species are fished at sustainable levels. In *Fishing for Solutions* Michael De Alessi provides an elegant explanation for this

---

[1] These figures come from the UNESCO web site http://www.unesco.org/opi/eng/98iyo/pl-ocean.htm; however, it is also noted there that most of the species remain undiscovered, so such estimates are mostly conjecture.

[2] *Ibid.*

[3] See the discussion of this issue below, p. 10.

phenomenon. Over-fishing typically occurs only where fishermen are not able to control their own destiny; when they do not know what proportion of future stocks they will own, they are disinclined to call for reduced catch levels because they do not know with any certainty that abstaining this year will bring them rewards in years to come. By contrast, where fishermen know that they are entitled to fish a certain proportion of the future catch, they are more likely to favour sustainable catch rates. Like shareholders in joint-stock companies, they have a strong incentive to encourage growth of fish stocks because they know that they will reap part of the benefits.

Most people argue that the solution to the problems faced by the world's fisheries is more government intervention. But the fact is that government intervention by and large caused the problem in the first place. More often than not catch levels are set and enforced by government officials who have no direct interest in ensuring the sustainability of the oceans' resources. Governments even subsidise over-fishing by providing grants for procuring better boats and nets.

Mr De Alessi is particularly critical of the European Common Fisheries Policy (CFP), which 'neatly condenses just about everything that is wrong with government management of the fisheries' (p. 35). Catch levels in the CFP are set according to the vagaries of political interests, with officials from each country trying to get the best deal for 'their' fishermen, regardless of the effects on stocks. Enforcement is bedevilled by distrust and perverse incentives. The lack of positive incentives leads fishermen to throw back over-quota fish or land illegally, and fishermen resist attempts by national authorities to impose surveillance systems because they know that trawlers landing illegally-caught fish in other nations' ports will be able to avoid capture. Even the philosophical basis upon which the CFP is founded, the idea of greater access, is contrary to good fisheries management, which requires exclusivity.

Where management of fish stocks has been devolved to the fishermen themselves, allowable catch levels have been set more appropriately and in most cases stocks have been fished sustainably. When given the opportunity of effectively owning the resource upon which they rely for their living, fishermen

6

have been much more willing conservationists because they know that what they save today will be theirs tomorrow.

The IEA Environment Unit has championed the introduction of private property rights as a mechanism for ensuring that individuals have a greater incentive to conserve resources, from deserts and wetlands to elephants and rhinos.[4] This book emphasises the rôle secure ownership can play in conserving fish and other marine resources. Mr De Alessi discusses the possibility of privatising certain areas of sea, allowing exclusive access only to certain individuals or groups of individuals. Where such exclusive ownership rights exist, such as in Japan's coastal fisheries, we see a greater profusion of artificial reefs, which seem to act as spawning grounds for fish. In these and other areas where the right to fish is owned privately by communities, strict rules have evolved that regulate the amount of fish that is caught.

An alternative property-rights solution which may be more applicable in regions where the fishermen no longer form a tight-knit homogeneous group, is to create Individually Transferable Quotas (ITQs). ITQs are rights to a specific share of the annual catch of a certain species in a certain area. Several such schemes exist around the world, the most successful of which is in New Zealand, where management of the ITQ system is devolving to fisheries management companies, who are directly responsible to the fishermen. Since the introduction of the ITQ system in New Zealand in 1986, most fish stocks have increased and the fishermen no longer need government subsidies to keep going. Other ITQ systems have been less successful because rights to the quota are less secure and governments continue to make decisions about the size of the total catch. The closer an ITQ system comes to being a system of private property rights, the better it serves both the fishermen and the environment.

The prognosis for the world's fisheries is not as gloomy as many commentators have made out but nor is it as rosy as some cornucopians pretend. Most likely, fisheries management will

---

[4] Julian Morris, *The Political Economy of Land Degradation*, IEA, 1995; Mark Pennington, *Conservation and the Countryside*, IEA, 1996; Ike Sugg and Urs Kreuter, *Elephants and Ivory: Lessons from the Trade Ban*, IEA, 1994; Michael 't Sas-Rolfes, *Rhinos: Conservation, Economics and Trade-offs*, IEA, 1995.

gradually evolve towards more sustainable practices. If they follow Mr De Alessi's advice they will arrive there more quickly.

As with all Institute publications, the views expressed in this monograph are those of the author, not of the Institute (which has no corporate view), its Trustees, Advisers or Directors. It is published as an important contribution to the debate on fisheries policy.

Julian Morris
Assistant Director, IEA Environment Unit

The Author

Michael De Alessi is a research associate at the Competitive Enterprise Institute and co-ordinator of the Center for Private Conservation in Washington, DC. He specialises in marine conservation issues. He received a BA in Economics and an MS in Engineering and Economic Systems from Stanford University and an MA in Marine Policy from the Rosenstiel School of Marine and Atmospheric Science at the University of Miami. In 1994 he was a research fellow at the Political Economy Research Center in Montana. He is the author of the IEA Environment Unit Working Papers 'Emerging Technologies and the Private Stewardship of Marine Resources' and 'Private Reef Building: Two Case Studies'. His articles on marine conservation have appeared in such publications as the *Wall Street Journal Europe*, *International Herald Tribune*, and *New Scientist*.

Acknowledgements

The paper would not have been possible without the tireless efforts of Julian Morris and Lisa Mac Lellan at the Institute of Economic Affairs and the intellectual support of the Competitive Enterprise Institute, in particular, Jonathan Adler's always-insightful comments and Fred Smith's optimism and encouragement. I would also like to thank Jim Seagraves and three anonymous referees for their numerous helpful suggestions. Finally and most importantly, I thank my parents, grandmother and Rachel Glitz for their heartfelt support.

M.D.A.

Introduction

Stories of fisheries collapse frequently grab the spotlight in the popular press. Sometimes these claims are exaggerated, sometimes not. In recent years the Food and Agriculture Organisation of the United Nations (FAO) has released figures describing the health of the world's fisheries, inevitably followed by a great hue and cry that the world's fisheries are on the verge of collapse. Fortunately, this is not the case, although there certainly has been a significant and disturbing decline in many important fish stocks over the years. Even so, the 1994 FAO figures suggested that less than 25 per cent of fish stocks were over-exploited, while approximately 44 per cent were being fully exploited (i.e. harvested at the maximum sustainable level). These are obviously vast generalisations – any attempt to describe the state of the world's oceans is a daunting and confusing task and is likely to be open to misinterpretation. However, some environmental organisations looking to present gloomier but more press-worthy facts drew attention to the finding that 'over seventy-five per cent of the world's fish stocks were either depleted, over-exploited or fully exploited' (FAO, 1994). The World Wildlife Fund, for example, recently claimed that 'Nearly everywhere fisheries have suffered catastrophic declines' and 'Without a doubt we have exceeded the limits of the seas'(Associated Press, 1996). Greenpeace seems to believe that due to overfishing, 'nature's balance is being altered across vast areas of the world's oceanic ecosystems in ways that may be irreversible'(Greenpeace, 1996). Of course, there is also a rosier view – using the same figures, one might claim that over 75 per cent of the world's fisheries are either fully, moderately or under-exploited.

Some species of fish certainly have suffered serious decline in some areas. For example, the cod stocks off New England and the Atlantic coast of Canada, once one of the world's richest fishing grounds, are now so depleted that they are close to commercial extinction.[1] But whilst it is tempting to extrapolate from this example, that would be a mistake. Many of the world's fish stocks are actually quite healthy. Moreover, fish stocks have been shown to be generally resilient – there is rarely any economic return to fishing out a stock below its biologically reproductive minimum (Myers *et al.*, 1995).

A significant problem is that of exaggeration, which results in a polarisation of the debate. Economist Julian Simon claims that 'No limit to the harvest of wild varieties of seafood is in sight' (Simon, 1996, p. 104). Whilst this obviously goes too far, environmentalists also warp the evidence to garner attention. The fact is that the world harvest of marine species has risen slowly in the last few years, but the increase has come primarily from harvests of lower value species and the discovery of new stocks. The primary cause of the exaggeration that characterises this polarised debate is the failure to pay attention to a vital piece of the puzzle: the role of institutions – the laws and social norms that constrain the behaviour of individuals and groups. It is self-evident that if the incentives created by these institutions favour unhampered extraction of fish from the sea, then the prospect for marine life will be bleak. If, on the other hand, the institutions provide incentives for conservation and stewardship, then the outlook for fish stocks will be much brighter.

In reality, the performance of fisheries varies from fish to fish and from place to place. It is particularly interesting to compare the health of stocks of the same species in different locations. Stocks of cod in the waters off Iceland and Norway have grown over the past few years, following serious declines during the early 1980s. At the same time, British fishermen have been fighting attempts by the European Commission to reduce their catches of dwindling cod stocks and the Canadian government announced that cod stocks off the Atlantic coast have fallen to a record low. What causes these disparities in how some countries manage successful fisheries whilst others simply languish in turmoil?

This paper attempts to provide answers to these questions by

---

[1] Commercial extinction occurs when it is not economically viable to catch the remaining fish.

analysing the different ways in which fish are managed around the world. It looks at the means by which individuals can be encouraged to manage marine resources sustainably, focusing on the role of institutions, conceptualised within the framework of the economics of property rights.

This property rights framework assumes that individuals act rationally under the constraints that they face. In particular, it asserts that constraints on the ability to use, benefit from and exchange resources are crucial elements of conservation. Chapter 1 develops such a property rights model in the context of marine resource management and suggests that the reason why some fisheries succeed while others fail is primarily related to the structure of ownership and control over those resources, which in turn affects the incentives for conservation. Chapter 2 discusses the reasons for the failure of certain fisheries management régimes, focusing particular attention on the European Common Fisheries Policy. Chapter 3 analyses one particularly successful example, that of New Zealand, showing how changes in management régimes followed from changes in the structure of ownership. Chapter 4 discusses the benefits of new technologies and alternative institutional structures (in particular, the importance of decentralised ownership and management) for the marine environment in general. Chapter 6 summarises the findings of the work and provides policy implications.

1. Property Rights, Economics and Marine Resources

Aristotle noted that 'those things which are owned by the greatest number of people are the least well cared for' (Politics ii). The argument is that if someone is going to share the return from any investment (such as efforts to conserve a resource), then they will tend to 'free ride' on the good will of others by making the least effort possible. For resource conservation this implies that in the absence of institutional constraints, each user will tend to extract as much as possible, regardless of the consequences. There will be little or no attempt to conserve the resource because each individual will know that whatever is left behind is simply likely to be taken by another.[2]

When the ocean's resources are free for the taking, the only way to benefit from them is by extraction. This does not cause problems when fish are plentiful and catches are small, but as the pressure on a fishery grows, so does the potential for depletion. Fishers realise that what they leave behind may simply be caught by someone else, and without any way to benefit from leaving fish in the water, they try to harvest as much as possible. This reduces fish populations and harms the fishery but, since the harmful effects of each fisher's actions are shared by all the participants, they are ignored (at least in the short term). Catching so many fish that the resource becomes depleted and the livelihood of the fishers destroyed may not make sense when looked at in aggregate, but on an individual level it makes perfect

---

[2] This scenario has come to be known as the 'Tragedy of the Commons', following a famous essay by Garret Hardin (1968) (who drew on the earlier work of economists like Gordon, 1954, and Scott, 1955). Unfortunately, Hardin did not initially recognise the efficacy of some institutions, particularly communal ones, and so his use of the word 'commons' has been the source of some confusion. Indeed, recent evidence suggests that the extent of free riding depends on numerous factors, the most crucial of which is the set of rules governing the way in which the resource is managed and the costs of monitoring and enforcing those rules. Ostrom (1990) discusses numerous examples of commons in which free riding is rare. The real problem seems to be not with commons *per se* but with resources that are not privately owned – that is either 'open access' and free to all or controlled by the state.

sense. In such a system of open access to a valuable resource with low harvesting costs, there are no rewards for restraint and the individually rational option is to fish at an unsustainable rate. Thus ruin is inevitable.

In order to understand the reasons for poor conservation of marine resources, it is helpful to understand the reasons for poor conservation in general. Fundamental to this is an understanding of the rôle of economic incentives and the importance of property rights.

Property Rights

Property rights are bundles of rights to such things as the use of a resource, the income derived from a resource, and the ability to transfer part or all of these rights (L. De Alessi, 1980). The structure of property rights affects behaviour because it establishes different allocations of benefits and harms among individuals. Any attempt to exert control over a resource is an attempt to define property rights in that resource, whether through regulation, a group rule or a form of exclusive ownership.

When no property rights are assigned, the situation is termed 'open access', but this is rare. Usually, property rights are either controlled by government, held in common by a group, or parcelled out among individuals. There is, of course, a great deal of overlap among these groups.[3]

It is important to note the effect of different property rights structures on resource use and conservation. Open access typically results in a total failure on the part of resource users to internalise the external costs and benefits of their behaviour.

---

[3] Unfortunately, Hardin lumped many different institutions into his definition of the commons. As examples of the tragedy of the commons, he cited airsheds, congested national parks, and medieval English grazing commons. This led to some confusion as each of these is governed by a very different set of institutional arrangements. Airsheds most closely resemble open access (although they need not necessarily be so – see Coase, 1960 and Rothbard, 1982), while national parks in the United States are government controlled and many medieval commons more closely resembled group ownership, complete with rules and restrictions for improved management (McCloskey, 1972 and Hanna, 1990). For many people, particularly anthropologists, the word 'commons' connotes exactly the opposite of what Hardin implied – strictly monitored use and access to a resource (Berkes *et al.*, 1989).

Even more common is a partial failure to internalise these externalities, as resource users respond to perverse incentives created by government intervention. As a result, these rewards and costs are discounted or ignored, and the resource generally suffers.

Open Access

'Ruin is the destination toward which all men rush, each pursuing his own best interest in a society that believes in the freedom of the commons. Freedom in a commons brings ruin to all.' *Garret Hardin (1968, p. 1,244)*

A completely open access régime is a free-for-all. In a fishery, there would be no limits on who may fish, the gear they may use or how many fish they may catch. While open access will frequently result in over-harvesting of resources, this is not necessarily the case. If there is little demand for a resource, that is, when demand is low relative to supply, open access may even be optimal. Devising rules or restrictions on behaviour is costly and if they have little or no effect on the health of a fishery, or are too costly to enforce, they may not be worth the effort.

Until recently many people thought that ocean fisheries were inexhaustible, and with the fishing gear available up until the end of the last century that was probably true. Imposing restrictions at that time would have made no sense; open access was rational.

Even as a resource begins to suffer from increased exploitation, open access may still be optimal for the very same reason. Often, keeping outsiders away from a resource is simply not feasible (see for example Demsetz, 1967; Libecap, 1989). However, as a resource increases in value it becomes more worthwhile to impose restrictions on its use.

Private Ownership

'A primary function of property rights is that of guiding incentives to achieve a greater internalization of externalities.' *Harold Demsetz (1967, p. 348)*

Property rights encourage the internalisation of the harms and benefits caused by a particular user or group of users because they determine whether the future effects of current behaviour (either positive or negative) will be borne by the owner. Thus, as property rights become better defined, resource stewardship becomes more attractive and, equally, owners bear more of the costs of rapacious behaviour.

The crucial determinant for the private ownership of a resource is that the welfare of the decision-makers is tied to the economic consequences of their decisions (L. De Alessi, 1980). Thus private property can take the form of either group or individual ownership – as long as the owners can exclude others, transfer ownership, decide how to manage a resource and bear the consequences, it is a private arrangement. However, terminology again causes some confusion. Property rights parcelled out to individuals or held jointly with others are typically referred to as private property rights and common property rights, respectively. However, as Elinor Ostrom and Margaret McKean (1995, p. 6) point out: 'It is crucial to recognise that common property is *shared private property*.'[4]

Throughout this paper, Ostrom and McKean's definition of common property is used – that is to say, common property rights are conceived as a private arrangement. Unfortunately, the terms private property and private property rights are generally accepted in the economics literature to refer to parcelled, individual rights, so to avoid confusion that definition will remain. It is important to note, however, that references to private ownership or private arrangements in the paper encompass both parcelled and communally owned property rights régimes.

Individually parcelled private property rights offer the greatest rewards for conservation to their owners, but are also the most costly to define and enforce. Thus, under a host of scenarios, common property may be optimal.

Common Property Rights

'It is one thing to contemplate the inshore sea from land's end as a stranger, to observe an apparently empty, featureless, open accessed

---

[4] In other sources common property does not have this definition, such as when it is used to refer to state managed resources. These resources may be managed as a common, but they are surely not private.

expanse of water. The image in a fisherman's mind is something very different. Seascapes are blanketed with history and imbued with names, myths, and legends, and elaborate territories that sometimes become exclusive provinces partitioned with traditional rights and owners much like property on land.' *John Cordell (1989, p. 1)*

Common property rights may assume many different forms, but essentially they define the rights shared by the members of a group with exclusive access to a resource (Ciriacy-Wnatrup and Bishop, 1980). They are often an effective way to internalise the benefits of conservation. McKean and Ostrom (1995, p. 6) provide an explanation for the existence of common property:

'Common property régimes are a way of privatizing the rights to something without dividing it into pieces ... Historically, common property régimes have evolved in places where the demand on a resource is too great to tolerate open access, so property rights in resources have to be created, but some other factor makes it impossible or undesirable to parcel the resource itself.'

In other words, common property régimes reward the group with many of the benefits of parcelled ownership without so many of the costs.

Because they rely on group control, common property régimes are often most effective among homogeneous groups of people, such as the close-knit Portuguese immigrant fishing communities in the north-eastern United States and the lobstermen mentioned below. Rules are easier to enforce in such a group because behaviour tends to be more predictable and sanctions are easier to levy. In some cases social ostracism or even mere disapproval is enough to warrant compliance with the rules.

Common property can be optimal under a number of conditions, ranging from nearly open access to a system of strict controls and rules (for a detailed analysis, see Ostrom, 1990). The level of control typically depends on the balance between the value of the resource and the costs of monitoring the group and excluding outsiders. A heterogeneous group makes it more difficult to reach agreements and therefore more difficult to manage resources. Differences among group members can range from attitudes toward risk and discount rates to simply how well people get along with each other. Thus restrictions on group

17

membership are quite common, and when outsiders are able to force access, these régimes are very often stressed.

One advantage of common property arrangements is risk sharing (McCloskey, 1972). The population dynamics of marine resources can be highly unpredictable, for example due to uncertain patterns of recruitment. Limiting oneself to a small area in this case would be very risky. Ostrom has pointed out that

'When no physical or institutional mechanisms exist for sharing risk, communal property arrangements may enable individuals to adopt productive activities not feasible under individual property rights' (Ostrom, 1997).

Common property régimes occur frequently in developing nations, where the relative value of fish tends to be higher, leading to greater competition for their capture and making monitoring and enforcement difficult. Parcelling resources into individual units under such circumstances is often not practicable, whereas vesting group control over a resource may be.

Lobsters

One valuable species that lends itself well to common property control is the lobster. In some of these cases, common property régimes arise where private ownership is not a legal option. In the Maine lobster fishery, the lobstermen have formed 'harbor gangs' that mark territories and turn away outsiders – an extra-legal common property arrangement (Acheson, 1987). As a result, lobstermen in these gangs have higher catches, larger lobsters, and larger incomes than lobstermen who fish outside controlled areas (Acheson, 1987). These gangs are often composed of members of a particular family or of long-standing community membership – exemplifying the importance of homogeneity to successful common property régimes.

In certain regions in Mexico, for example around Cozumel and Punta Allen, some fishery co-operatives have created common property régimes that limit access to the lobster fishery and assign rights to specific areas to specific fishers (Miller, 1989, and Seijo, 1993). Members of these co-operatives set rules and restrictions on lobster harvests and enforce territorial boundaries called *campos* that are divided within the co-operative. Within these campos many fishers create artificial habitats for the lobsters – called *casitas* around Cozumel and *sombras* in Punta Allen – that are believed to make fishing easier and more productive by concentrating the lobsters and by reducing non-human predation. In areas to the North where there are no campos, lobster populations are commonly depleted, and no one maintains any artificial habitats for the lobsters.

Even in the United Kingdom the stage is being set for the private ownership of some lobster grounds. A new law which received royal assent in 1997 will make it an offence to take lobsters deliberately placed on the sea bed by fishers in designated areas up to six miles from the shore (Brown, 1997). Lobster ranching projects have already started in the Orkneys and Shetlands, and research has shown that if young lobsters evade predation, recapture rates should average 50 per cent (Brown, 1997).

Coral Reefs

Coral reefs in the South Pacific have suffered of late from destructive fishing practices such as fishing with dynamite or cyanide. However, such practices are often proscribed in places where fishing rights are securely owned, most often by a village, clan or community. Biologist Robert Johannes studied coral reef conservation throughout the Pacific and found village control over local marine resources to be the surest indicator of reef health (Johannes and Ripen, 1996). This finding highlights one of the most important attributes of successful common property management of marine resources: secure tenure.

Reef tenure typically takes the form of ownership by a clan, chief or family, and often extends from the beach to the outer edge of the reef, sometimes even miles out to sea (M. De Alessi, 1997a). These reefs are valuable assets to the community and so are fiercely protected. In Fiji some communities employ fish wardens to watch over the reefs. In Johannes's study of Palauan fishers, he found community-managed fisheries employing closed seasons and areas, abiding by size limits and even imposing quotas to ensure conservation (Johannes, 1981).

The experience in much of the Philippines offers a dramatic contrast. Most of the common property régimes there were destroyed by the Spanish Conquest and today fishing over much of the reefs is nearly open access and many reefs there are dead or deteriorating. The World Wildlife Fund's Hong Kong office has looked into the problem of cyanide fishing and found that reef fisheries in Southeast Asia 'work in a sustainable way only in those few places where the rights to fish a particular reef are clearly established' (*The Economist*, 11 May 1996, p. 35).

Japanese Co-operatives
In Japan the rights to coastal marine resources are frequently held by Fishery Co-operative Associations (FCAs). These associations have clearly defined rights recognised by Japanese law. Ironically, co-operative ownership of near-shore waters was created under feudalism as a basis for levying taxes but today FCAs are the beneficiaries of huge subsidies (Christy, 1997).

FCAs impose strict conservation measures on their members and coastal marine resources in Japan are generally healthy. Co-operative ownership in Japan is so strong that FCAs have even been able to block potentially harmful or polluting coastal development (Jeffreys, 1996). As noted, these co-operatives are hardly private, but they do offer an emphatic demonstration that exclusive control leads to the stewardship of marine resources.

European Common Property Régimes
Although not nearly as strong as in Japan, there is also a legacy of fishery co-operatives in Europe. In France, there is a long history of self-regulation by the local Prud'homies, groups following an ancient tradition of fraternal organisation of vessel owners in each port. Elected officers called Prud'hommes settle disputes and set restrictions on fishing practices, and traditionally have had legislative, enforcement, and judicial functions (Pearse, 1980). These Prud'homies were even able to limit the bountiful harvests (and therefore potentially low prices) that followed the resumption of fishing after the Second World War (Pearse, 1980).

Similar organisations exist in Spain and are called Cofradias. In 1980 there were Cofradias in all 60 Spanish fishing ports on the Mediterranean coast (Pearse, 1980). Although membership was voluntary, every fisher, both owner and crew, joined. Among other things, Cofradias regulated fishing and organised the sale of fish.

Italian fishery co-operatives on the Adriatic have also enjoyed some success. In the early 1970s they were able to raise their catches by restricting the days each fisher could spend at sea (Pearse, 1980). In fact, they liked this limit on fishing so much that soon afterwards they successfully shortened the fishing week to less than four days.

Private Property Rights

Private property rights offer the greatest rewards for conservation, but at a higher cost. Clearly defined and readily enforceable private property rights to marine resources are rare. However, those few examples that do exist strongly support the arguments of theorists who have promoted private property rights in the oceans as a means to improve resource management (see, for example, Keen, 1983, Scott, 1988a, Jeffreys, 1996, and Edwards, 1994).

In order to be effective, private property rights must be well defined, enforceable, and transferable (Anderson and Leal, 1991). Although some common property régimes include a measure of alienation, transferability is generally what sets private property apart from common property. Transferability is crucial for owners to capitalise on the value of their assets, to use them as collateral and to capture the future returns that stem from investments.

Private property rights reduce, but do not eliminate, the effects of heterogeneity on resource management. Heterogeneous owners will still have difficulties reaching agreement, but private property rights make contracting easier, which in turn facilitates working around these differences (see Johnson and Libecap, 1982). Even fully allocated and transferable rights often have a common property component to them – limits, quotas, etc. that are mutually agreed. Only when the harvesting activity of one individual has *no* effect on other harvesters does heterogeneity cease to matter.

Stronger private rights mean that more benefits and harms are internalised by the owner of a resource. Thus, as private property rights are more effectively defined and enforced, the welfare of the owner and the consequences of his activities grow more

21

closely related (L. De Alessi, 1980).

Oysters

One of the few empirical studies of the effects of private property rights on marine resources was done in the 1970s by Richard Agnello and Lawrence Donnelley (1975), economists at the University of Delaware. They looked at oyster beds in the Chesapeake Bay (in Maryland and Virginia) and in some of the states on the Gulf of Mexico. They compared those managed by state regulators to those owned by private leaseholders and found that the leased oyster beds were healthier, better maintained, and produced better quality oysters.

This difference in performance occurred because leaseholders were spared the fear that someone else might harvest the oysters before they did, so they invested in protecting their oysters and enhancing oyster habitat. One way they did this was to spread old oyster shells on their beds, providing an ideal substrate on which larval oysters could settle. On the public oyster beds, no such steps were taken voluntarily. The private property rights rewarded stewardship and innovation and thereby encouraged individuals to protect and enhance fishery resources.

England and France demonstrate a similar dichotomy of approaches to managing their oyster fisheries (see Neild, 1995). Both countries had some history of private ownership of near-shore areas until they were subsumed by the monarchy many centuries ago. In England, the monarchy took this opportunity to make most oyster beds open to the public, and declines in production soon resulted. Oysters had been commonplace in England up to this point, and during the time of Dickens were a staple of the poor. But by the time the first official statistics were compiled in 1886, the number of oysters had fallen precipitously. To make matters worse, a Royal Commission charged with looking into the matter recommended that same year that all restrictions on sea fisheries should be removed, and they subsequently were. A later report did correctly cite over-dredging in open waters as the reason for the decline in oyster harvests, but it was ignored and harvests continued to suffer.

Oyster harvests in France suffered a similar decline in the late 19th century, but the response was very different. The monarchy used its control over the foreshore to grant concessions to favoured subjects. While there certainly was some government assistance for the development of the oyster fishery, the sense of ownership engendered by these exclusive concessions resulted in a healthy industry. Today there are about 200 oysters produced in France for every one in Great Britain (Neild, 1995).

Although the benefits and feasibility of private property rights are most readily apparent for sedentary species like oysters, they are perfectly applicable to more far-ranging species as well. They have in fact been applied to salmon and are beginning to evolve even for some offshore fisheries (both examples are discussed in later sections).

The Evolution of Property Rights

How and why private property rights develop depends on the value of resources and the costs of monitoring them. As the former increases and/or the latter decreases, the benefits of private ownership increase and, in a favourable institutional setting, an open access régime will give way to a private (common or parcelled) one. This process is circular; as resources become more valuable owners invest more in monitoring and enforcing private ownership rights, which in turn makes resources more valuable, and so on.

As noted earlier, open access may be an optimal approach. Ostrom (1990, p. 40) notes that 'the costs involved in transforming a situation from one in which individuals act independently to one in which they coordinate activities can be quite high'. For Steven Cheung (1970), the progression towards private arrangements depends primarily on the costs of excluding outsiders, regulating insiders and enforcing private rights. Thus, the institutional arrangements that develop are a measure of the balance between the gains from asserting rights to valuable resources and the costs of heterogeneity on co-operation and enforcement. Of course, the nature of the resource also plays an important role. Sedentary species such as oysters are easier to monitor and protect than free-swimming, far-ranging species such as tuna.

An early example of the development of private ownership rights concerned the trade in beaver pelts and the Montagne

23

Indians in North America (Demsetz, 1967). Prior to the arrival of the settlers, beavers were plentiful and not highly valued by the Montagne, and so they did not bother to impose any restrictions on harvesting them. But with the rise of the fur trade, the value of beaver pelts increased rapidly and suddenly the beavers became susceptible to depletion. The Montagne responded by rapidly developing a system for allocating certain areas to specific families who could then benefit from conserving the beaver. As beaver were the only resource valuable enough to warrant this kind of protection there were no other harvest restrictions imposed on these territories; other people were free to roam across them and were even free to kill and eat the beaver as long as they left the pelt behind.

The American West

At the end of the 19th century, land in the American West seemed boundless and plentiful. Much like the oceans not so long ago, one could hardly imagine depleting its vast resources. But as the West was settled, its water and grassy lands became progressively more scarce and more valuable. Research by economists Terry Anderson and P.J. Hill (1975) has shown that, as the rights to these resources became more valuable, more effort went into enforcing private property rights, and therefore into innovation and resource conservation.

Defining private property by physical barriers was desirable, but initially in the West there were too few raw materials for this to be possible, so livestock intermingled and monitoring was difficult. However, frontier entrepreneurs soon developed branding systems to identify individual animals, and organisations such as cattlemen's associations were formed to standardise and register these brands. These branding technologies allowed cattlemen to define and enforce private property rights over a valuable roaming resource.

Then in the 1870s another innovation came along that radically altered the frontier landscape – barbed wire. Barbed wire was an inexpensive and effective means of marking territory, excluding interlopers, and keeping in livestock. It became easier to enclose property and exert private ownership. Innovations such as barbed wire that developed during the westward expansion of the 1800s illustrate how private property rights encourage innovation.

Similar challenges to those faced by the early settlers in the American West are faced today in the oceans. It is often difficult to envision alternative methods of managing natural resources, especially in the marine environment, but wherever private property rights may be asserted, incentives exist to develop methods of fencing and branding no matter what the physical environment.

From Common to Private Property

Common property rights evolve much like private property rights. Ostrom and McKean (1995, p. 8) have pointed out that 'Creating a common property régime may be a way of instituting collective management rules – which function as imaginary fences and informal courts' in cases where it is not practicable to create a formal court system and/or where some form of 'barbed wire' would be very costly.

There are also many cases where common property rights have evolved smoothly into private property rights. In the Marovo Lagoon in the Solomon Islands, for example, a number of well-defined clans control resources both on land and in the water (Hviding, 1991). Recently, as giant clams have grown scarcer and more valuable in the region, the prospect of giant clam aquaculture has produced a variety of new marine tenure arrangements, including the zoning of reefs and their allocation to individual families (Hviding, 1991).

In Japan, co-operative arrangements have shown an amazing ability to adapt to changing circumstances, most likely due to their formal recognition under the law. Some land co-operatives have even leased out large areas for the development of golf courses (McKean and Ostrom, 1995).

When the lobster fishers of Punta Allen, Mexico, were given exclusive access to the lobster fishery in their area, the co-operatives not only developed strict internal rules to moderate behaviour and to ensure conservation; they also divided this area up into 150 lots (Seijo, 1993). Rights to these areas are transferable within the community and new entrants to the fishery are not uncommon.

In the mountain village of Törbel, Switzerland, which has successfully managed a grazing commons since the Middle Ages, both common and private property rights have evolved simultaneously (Ostrom, 1990). For the commons the village has absolute rules on the transfer of rights and the use of these resources, which include grazing meadows, forests, paths and roads. However, the villagers also have private lots to grow grains, fruits, vegetables, and hay for the winter.

Common property rights remain when parcelling them is difficult and/or the returns from them are low. Otherwise, as resources grow in value and/or monitoring becomes cheaper, private property rights become increasingly attractive (Demsetz, 1967).

2. The Tragedy of Government Intervention

'Some [common property régimes] may have disappeared naturally as communities opted for other arrangements, particularly in the face of technological and economic change, but in most instances common property régimes seem to have been legislated out of existence.' *Margaret McKean and Elinor Ostrom (1995, p. 3)*

Perhaps the greatest weakness of common property régimes is their lack of resiliency in the face of pressure from outsiders. There are two main reasons for this. First, common property systems are often informal agreements not recognised by the courts. Their owners often have no legal recourse when their resources are threatened or simply taken by force. Second, because common property rights are often not alienable, out-transfers may not be possible (Ostrom, 1997). As a result, pressure from outsiders for access often leads to expropriation, either of the resource itself or of the right of access to it.

Common property régimes in Japan have succeeded because they are formally recognised and very secure, which allows co-operatives both to defend their rights in court and to develop ways of accommodating out-transfers. Moreover, in both Swiss and Japanese common lands, the covenants regulating ownership often contain rules for parcelling out among individuals in case the rights become more valuable (Ostrom, 1990). A similar set of rules initially allowed the enclosure of common lands in England only when all owners of usufruct rights to the land agreed (McCloskey, 1972).

Unfortunately, in most places around the world, not only does the legal system not recognise common property rights, it is often biased against them. Many common property arrangements are simply not supported by the legal authorities when challenged by non-members (Ostrom, 1997). In fact, many legal systems favour private property at the expense of common property. This results in the elimination of collective landholdings and in the take-over of communal properties by individual proprietors (Ostrom, 1997).

Although expropriation by simple theft does occur, the most common form of expropriation is political. For example, in England the majority of commoners that was required in order to effect an enclosure was altered by Acts of Parliament in the 18th and 19th centuries: the original Common Law rule of unanimity was changed first to a rule of four-fifths majority and then to one of three-quarters majority (McCloskey, 1972). This problem is recognised by some supporters of artisanal fisheries, who argue that politics is the source of a great many fishing community problems. For example, an article in *The Ecologist* points out that 'those with political connections outside the community are increasingly able to circumvent the rules governing the fishing commons and to dominate the decision-making process' (Fairlie *et al.*, 1995, p. 50).

An interesting cycle of expropriation occurred with the arrival of settlers to the Pacific Northwest of the United States. Indigenous people there had developed complicated arrangements, both within and between tribes, to manage the salmon fisheries (see Higgs, 1982). Native Americans relied heavily on fixed nets and weirs along the riverbank but were careful to allow plenty of fish to pass in order to maintain the spawning runs and ensure a future supply. According to Robert Higgs (1982, p. 59),

'Indian regulation of the fishery, though varying from tribe to tribe, rested on the enforcement of clearly understood property rights. In some cases these rights rested in the tribe as a whole; in other cases in families or individuals.'

As settlers began to move into these areas, at first they respected these property right régimes and often traded peacefully with the Native Americans. But as their numbers and power increased, they quickly moved to expropriate the fisheries by force. Before long two very different methods of harvesting the salmon developed. Some of the new arrivals used fish wheels to harvest fish along the riverbanks mechanically while others used labour-intensive methods to chase down their prey at sea. Intra-settler expropriation soon followed. Sensing their great superiority of numbers, the hook-and-line fishers went to the ballot box and were able to have the more efficient fish wheels banned.

Government Regulation of Fisheries
Private property rights are much more likely to be recognised in courts of law and to be resilient to expropriation by force. Government regulation and intervention of other kinds, however, seem to pose an equally large threat to both private and common property rights régimes.

The reasons given for government intervention into fisheries management are myriad. They are normally couched in rhetoric about protecting 'the common heritage of mankind', but at the heart of the matter is usually the improvement of someone's welfare, whether it be a bureaucrat or a constituent.

Even the great proponent of the freedom of the seas, Hugo Grotius, had an ulterior motive. When he wrote his famous treatise, *Mare Liberum*, in the early 17th century, he proclaimed that the oceans and their resources were inexhaustible and demanded freedom of access for everyone. This sounded altruistic, but in reality Grotius, a Dutchman, was responding to attempts by the British navy, which was stronger than the Dutch, to control access to the high seas (Christy and Scott, 1965).

Sadly, little has changed since then. Grotius's ideas still hold sway amongst politicians and special interests alike and they continue to be used to justify open access to valuable resources. When some years ago it appeared that deep seabed mining might be lucrative, many developing nations claimed that these resources were part of the 'common heritage of mankind' and demanded their share (for a full discussion of this debate, and a property rights solution, see Denman, 1984).

The public choice literature has much to say about the motivations of public servants, well-meaning or not, to promote their own welfare by increasing their budget, the size and importance of their agency, and so on. For those who are being regulated the benefits are often even more obvious: restrictions on competition or access to previously unavailable resources, for example.

However, the problem is not so much public servants, but politics itself. The National Marine Fisheries Service (NMFS) in the United States regularly provides the best available scientific data on fish stocks, which in turn is routinely ignored by policy-makers. In contrast, a reduction in political wrangling explains some of the success of the North Pacific Fishery Management Council in the US. Alaskans dominate the council, but much of the fishing industry is based in Washington state. With most of the fishing constituency located in a different state, the Alaskans can afford to be much more impartial. In other words, the less exposure to political expediency, the less pressure to distort scientific advice. (But by the same token, any sort of rights-based fishing is vehemently opposed by the Alaskans for fear that much of the rights would be allocated to fishers in Washington.)

One of the most understandable rationales for government involvement comes from the fishers themselves. In cases where appropriate private institutions restricting access to and use of a resource are not developing, either because of the nature of the resource or because of the character of the community, shifting the costs of enforcement to some higher government authority may be attractive. In reality, however, it is unlikely that the benefits of this solution will outweigh the disadvantages of government control. The same forces that impede co-operation to exclude outsiders or to monitor resources prevent fishers from lobbying for effective rules and regulations (see Johnson and Libecap, 1982, and Karpoff, 1987). It is at least as difficult to agree on what form of government regulation to endorse as it is to agree on the creation of a system of private property.

One of the most common pretexts for government intervention is as a cure for 'market failure'. But market failure is not a failure of the market, but rather a failure to have markets. Often private institutions have not developed for good reason, and presupposing that government intervention will improve resource management in this case is a mistake. Rules and regulations promulgated externally are unlikely to internalise harms and benefits.

Maintaining open access does appeal to egalitarian values, but a shift to private ownership is more likely to ensure access to a valuable, plentiful resource, than would open access to a depleted wasteland. The greater the formal recognition for private arrangements, the easier it becomes for new entrants to lease or buy into a fishery. If there is no collateral in the fishery, entry becomes much more difficult. When a form of private property rights was instituted in New Zealand, researchers found almost immediately that 'transferability ... allowed fishers to enter and exit the fishery more easily' (Clark *et al.*, 1988, p. 331; see also Chapter 4 below).

The simplest explanation given for most government intervention into the fisheries is also often the most spurious: that it is in the best interests of those being regulated. In Mar-del-Plata, just south of Buenos Aires in Argentina, the fishing co-operative there placed severe effort restrictions on fishing to ensure a limited harvest, both for conservation and to fetch a better price for their fish at the market. But an earnest government agent in Buenos Aires figured out that the sustainable catch level was actually far higher so, ignoring the price effects of an increase in supply, he tried to convince the fishers of Mar-del-Plata to change their ways. It took a concerted effort to avoid this 'improvement' – the fishers caught as many fish as they could, then left them out to rot on the docks. Finally, the government was convinced that the fishers actually *could* catch more fish, they just didn't *want* to.[5]

The Effects of Government Regulation

'When resources that were previously controlled by local participants have been nationalized, state control has usually proved to be less effective and efficient than control by those directly affected, if not disastrous in its consequences.' *Elinor Ostrom (1997)*

Government regulation of the fisheries is pervasive world-wide and the results have generally been less than laudable. Waste of resources, time, effort and capital have not only been encouraged through regulation, but have also frequently been subsidised.

The most common forms of government regulation to date ignore the problem of open access and instead attempt to limit fishing harvests with restrictions on fishing gear, effort and seasons. This approach has resulted in the use of laughably outdated harvesting techniques, huge influxes of capital merely to subvert regulatory restrictions (known as overcapitalisation) and dangerous races to harvest fish, but little or no progress in

---

5   Francis Christy, personal communication, Autumn 1994.

stemming the depletion of fisheries. This adversarial relationship between the regulators and the fishers does little to discourage fishers from harvesting as many fish as possible – fishers are quite adept at staying one step ahead of the latest limitations imposed on them.

In order to circumvent regulations, fishers frequently make large investments in capital – buying bigger boats or larger nets, for example. Indeed, when Frederick Bell (1972, p. 156) studied the northern lobster fisheries in the United States in the 1970s, he estimated that 'over 50 per cent of the capital and labour employed in lobstering represent an uneconomic use of factors'. Attempts to avoid regulatory restrictions sometimes reach a comical extent. Restrictions on the length of boats leads to very wide boats; limits on the number of nets leads to bigger nets; short seasons lead to very fast boats or boats with more storage and freezer facilities on board. All inevitably lead to complaints that fisheries are overcapitalised.

The Alaskan halibut fishery was an extreme example of regulatory failure. As pressure on this fishery increased, regulators responded by shortening the seasons during which the fish could be caught. The fishing fleet responded predictably by finding ways to catch fish more quickly and before long the entire year's season had been shortened to just two days. The same amount of fish were caught as before, only now the fishery was a dangerous derby, held often in bad weather and with frequent loss of life. Not only that, but fresh fish were only available for a very short time, the fish were handled poorly in the rush and most fish went straight into the freezer, decreasing their value.

In other fisheries that have been depleted, a common government response is not to overhaul the regulatory régime but to bail out those affected. When the cod stocks off Canada's Atlantic coast crashed, the government in Ottawa responded by sending in huge sums of money but little in the way of substantive reform. They found it easier to buy everybody off than actually to deal with the problem. In 1992 it was estimated that subsidies to the fishing industry world-wide amounted to about \$54 billion (FAO, 1993a).[6] This is hardly an exact number, but it does give some idea of the large impact that subsidies have on the fishing industry world-wide. Even as fishery managers are realising that there are 'too many people chasing too few fish' and are trying to tackle this problem, subsidies often do the very opposite.

Another example of the perversity of government intervention is the effect of anti-trust law on the fisheries. Anti-trust law purports to protect consumers by preventing collusive activities that raise prices, but by discouraging co-operation, anti-trust undermines efforts to conserve stocks through the establishment of private arrangements (Yandle, 1997a). One such example is the Texas shrimp fishery (see Johnson and Libecap, 1982). In the 1950s the fishery was declining. Shrimpers were catching small, juvenile shrimp and prices were falling. The shrimpers responded by using their union to create something like a common property régime. The union limited entry into the fishery and set minimum size requirements for landed shrimp. As a result, larger shrimp were targeted and the health of the fishery improved. But other shrimpers who wanted to enter the fishery brought an anti-trust action against the union. The new entrants won, the harvesting free-for-all returned and the fishery fell back into decline.

It is unreasonable to expect a regulatory agency effectively to juggle the competing interests of a heterogeneous fishing industry, fish processors, environmentalists, and the regulators themselves (also a heterogeneous group). One of the worst aspects of this kind of system is that it is a zero-sum game. Political battles ensue over pieces of a pie that never gets bigger. Instead of investing in efforts to enlarge the pie, resources are devoted to attempts to grab a bigger piece of the same pie (or even a diminishing one) at some else's expense (Hide and Ackroyd, 1990).

Regulatory régimes also necessitate a one-size-fits-all approach whereby similar rules and restrictions are applied

---

6   According to Francis Christy (1996) this figure came from estimates of world-wide fishing costs and revenues and assumed that subsidies must account for a substantial portion of the difference between the two. It should be noted that in 1989 the fleet of the USSR made up a large proportion of total costs.

across the board, regardless of the varying circumstances of each fishery. This causes problems because every fishery is different and what works wonders in one may be woefully unsuited to another. Bureaucracies are reluctant to respond to these differences, however, as the rewards from a successful bureaucratic innovation pale in comparison to costs of not following procedure. Under most current systems, the only way to try a different approach is to cheat.

At the moment, fisheries scientists try to predict a total allowable harvest of fish by determining the maximum sustainable yield for any one species. This is a complicated task that includes tremendous uncertainties about such factors as migration patterns, feeding habits, fish recruitment, ideal rate and age to be harvested and inter-species relationships, all of which can fluctuate wildly from year to year. Even for species where records have been kept for centuries, scientists rarely predict fluctuations. Fisheries biologists admit that they are lucky if their population estimates for any one species are within 30 per cent of reality (Holmes, 1994).

Moreover, any system that ignores the *value* of fish is fundamentally flawed. Thus, the complexity of the underlying biological and physical systems precludes a reductionist approach to management. Optimum levels of exploitation must be determined by trial and error, and large levels of natural variability mask the effects of depletion, making it difficult to detect until it is severe (Ludwig *et al.*, 1993). This effect is only heightened by the purveyance of subsidies and regulatory régimes that bear most of the costs of these uncertainties. Much as the guarantee of government bailouts encouraged risky behaviour and eventual ruin in the savings and loan industry in the US, fishery managers and the industry err on the side of optimism, often until fish stocks have become depleted.

Further problems are caused because, once in place, regulatory régimes are very difficult to change. Even though current regulations may be detrimental to the fishery as a whole, some individuals will do well under them and will have a vested interest in maintaining the *status quo*. Any change in the rules will produce winners and losers, both real and perceived, and the losers will naturally resist the change. Nevertheless, government

34

involvement in the fisheries is constantly changing, sometimes for the better, mostly for the worse.

The Common Fisheries Policy

'I have never met a single fisherman who is pro-CFP.' *John Goodlad, Shetland Fisherman's Organisation (1995, p. 72)*

One of the most egregious examples of government involvement in fisheries management must be the European Common Fisheries Policy (CFP). Indeed, it neatly condenses just about everything that is wrong with government management of the fisheries. It is, not to put too fine a point on it, an unmitigated disaster.

Whilst governments in other countries move towards sustainable fishing policies based on limited access, the CFP has as one of its central objectives increased access to EU waters for member-states. If all goes according to current plan, all access restrictions on EU vessels will cease in the year 2002. Overall fishery quotas will continue to be set by the EU, but those quotas will be open to the licensed fishing vessels of any EU member-state.

Increased access is not the only problem. Typical regulatory perversities that already exist on a national level are multiplied in the EU Fisheries Commission. Wasteful subsidies run amok, conservation is ignored and opportunities to play the system abound.

The Common Fisheries Policy began in 1971, when the key issue was freedom of access to Community fishing grounds. The CFP assumed its current form in 1983. The objectives of the CFP are filled with vague egalitarian ideals that naturally have been interpreted to the advantage of each country involved and have led to a great deal of bickering between nations. Among the stated objectives of the CFP are 'to increase productivity by promoting technical progress' and to ensure 'optimal utilisation of the factors of production', 'a fair standard of living for the agricultural community' and 'supplies for consumers at reasonable prices' (Article 7 of the Common Fisheries Policy). It also promises to take into account the 'needs of both producers and consumers'.

In 1970, just prior to the original CFP agreement, the European Community formed the Common Structural Policy, which aimed to promote the construction and modernisation of coastal and pelagic fishing vessels and of the marketing and processing industry. With the introduction of the CFP, the Community adopted a new structural policy which quickly aimed to take advantage of the increased jurisdictions of most states out to 200 miles.

When Spain and Portugal joined the EC in 1985, they increased the number of fishing vessels in the Community by almost a third, so the structural policy was again revised at the end of 1986 (Karagiannakos, 1995). The revision increased subsidies for carrying out structural measures, encouraged fishing in the open ocean, and also began attempts to reduce fishing capacity within EC waters.

This 1986 regulation was slated to last for 10 years but survived for only five. In 1990 a new structural regulation increased funds for Spanish and Portuguese fleet improvements and added funds for 'small-scale, non-industrial' fishing vessels, one of the few classes so far overlooked for subsidisation. It did reduce some aid for building and modernisation, but increased mothballing funds and encouraged exploration of new fishing grounds.

The results of all these subsidies could easily have been predicted: too many fishing boats trying to catch too few fish. By 1994 it was estimated that the EU fleet could be cut by 40 per cent and still catch the same amount of fish (*The Economist*, 19 March, 1994). But subsidies to boat building and modernisation continued, as did efforts to *reduce* the number of fishing vessels, creating a sad, comic dance between opposing subsidies.

The first attempts to reduce fishing capacity failed miserably. Vessels were scrapped, but their licences were not, so fishing effort went unchanged and millions of pounds were spent for naught. In addition, the Commission accepted as withdrawals vessels sunk long before the 1986 regulation and accepted others in cases where there was no evidence given that the retired boats were even fishing vessels (Karagiannakos, 1995). The Court of Auditors found cases where Community aid was awarded for some projects even after their completion. In the end:

'Although the Community's principal objective [was] to reduce the fishing capacity of the fleet, the Community has ended up by granting more financial aid for the construction and modernisation of vessels than for the withdrawal over the years 1971 to 1990.' (Karagiannakos, 1995, p. 227).

To make matters worse, even though the stated goal of the programme is to remove the maximum number of productive vessels at the lowest cost, many of the boats that were removed were older, less productive boats, already headed for the scrap heap (Melhuish, 1995).

The other, equally unsuccessful attempt to conserve fish stocks has been the setting of catch quotas on individual species. These quotas are proposed by marine biologists and fisheries scientists and are ostensibly based on estimates of the sustainable catch level. They are then haggled over by politicians in Brussels who trade increases with one another without due regard to the impact on the health of the stocks. Finally, the quotas are often further undercut on the water by fishers ignoring their quotas and catching 'black' (unreported) fish. Estimates of the amount of fish caught illegally vary widely, but one senior UK fisheries inspector estimated that it was as high as 50 per cent of the legal quota on species like cod, making the recently proposed 12 per cent reduction in quota laughable (Clover, 1997).

One Commission mid-term report in 1991 admitted that there was little compliance with total allowable catches (TACs) and quotas anywhere in the Community (Karagiannakos, 1995). In November 1994 scientists from the International Council for the Exploration of the Seas (ICES) warned that the North Sea cod fishery was on the verge of collapse; four months later a huge (nearly 20 per cent) increase in the North Sea cod quota was announced (Fairlie, 1995). In 1995, ICES suggested a 40 per cent cut in the catch of hake and after much haggling EU ministers did finally agree to a cut – a whopping 5 per cent (Hagler, 1995).

It has been pointed out, quite correctly, that

'Almost every measure that the CFP has ever proposed has ... been subject to prolonged horse-trading as the fisheries ministers of individual member-states fight for the interests of their fishing industries (or, more accurately, those sectors of their industries with the greatest political influence).' (Fairlie, 1995, p. 108).

37

A successful EU fisheries minister is not one who helps ensure the future productivity of the stocks that nation's fishers depend on, but the one who can bring home the biggest slice of the resource pie.

For example, the political clout of the French fishing industry was on display in 1994 when French fishers responded to cheap fish imports from Russia and Poland by storming a Paris fish market and destroying about 60 tons of fish. The response? A £32 million aid package from the French government to appease them (Drozdiak, 1996).

Political savvy has also played its part in the UK, where fisheries are still largely divided along the lines set out years ago between those fishing for cod or herring (Fairlie, 1995). Herring are caught in deeper water offshore and require much larger boats and capital investments concentrated in a small number of ports. With fewer participants and large investments at stake, they are better organised, and while they may dislike the CFP, they have benefited from it. The herring fleet has had a relatively stable EU quota, while smaller groups have seen UK quotas fluctuate and consequently feel that their interests have been sold out in Brussels (Fairlie, 1995). The cod fishery, which now targets all sorts of whitefish (cod, haddock, plaice, sole, etc.) consists of many relatively small boats scattered throughout the country. It is these smaller, less well-organised interests who see almost no benefit from the CFP, indeed many support withdrawal.

Not surprisingly, the CFP is widely regarded as a failure (Karagiannakos, 1995). There may be little hope that the CFP can be salvaged, but there is hope that EU fisheries officials might at least recognise that the only way forward is to promote private arrangements to conserve marine resources. The CFP has failed because its creators did not understand the difference between open markets and open access. Whilst the former is desirable the latter certainly is not. The surest way both to help EU fishers and to guarantee access to foreign fishing grounds is not by expropriating access rights and subjecting resources to the tragedy of government regulation, but by formally recognising private rights and allowing international trade, of both products and the resources themselves.

To some these trades will probably sound like the quota-hopping problem that has lately been the bane of UK fishers, but there is an important difference. Quota hopping is, quite simply, when foreign interests (in this case usually the Spanish) buy UK quotas and proceed to fish, legally, in otherwise off-limits UK waters. The quotas that are bought by outsiders only have an access value. There is little they can do to influence the management of the fishery and so their quotas have little or no tie to the health of the fishery. Thus, they have little incentive to take any interest in conservation, especially since access is expected to increase in 2002. If quotas were real private property rights, however, it would clearly be against the self-interest of individual fishers to deplete the fishery in this way.

In fact, some UK fish producers' organisations – created initially to co-ordinate sales and administer EC price controls (Leal, 1996) – are already in the business of allocating the EU quotas they receive to their members. It would not be too difficult to vest these organisations with the right to set, monitor and enforce quota levels. A number of non-EU states have in fact started to move in this direction and the results so far have been promising (see Chapter 3).

Sadly, the EU does not appear to have any interest in moving towards a system of private ownership of marine resources. The current Fisheries Commissioner, Emma Bonino, apparently does not understand the relationship between institutions, opportunity and conservation. At a press conference in October 1996, she said:

'We believe that market forces alone would impose a law of the jungle leading to an unequal decimation of fleets and above all a decimation of stocks which could never be reversed'. (Reuters, 1996).

The outlook for reform does not look rosy.

3. Getting the Institutions Right

'It's the first group of fishers I've ever encountered who turned down the chance to take more fish.' *Philip Major, New Zealand Ministry of Agriculture*[7] *(quoted in The Economist, 1994, p. 24)*

In contradistinction to the goals of the Common Fisheries Policy, many countries are beginning to experiment with more private approaches to fisheries management. The most common tool to date for this is the Individual Transferable Quota (ITQ), which grants the owner the right to harvest a certain amount of fish in a given year, and can be bought or sold. ITQs have been introduced in recent years in New Zealand, Iceland, Australia, the United States and Canada.

ITQs are not real private property rights, but they are often a step in the right direction. In contrast to regulation-based government controls, they are incentive-compatible, vesting those who harvest the resource with some incentive to conserve the fishery. They also offer a real opportunity to begin to move towards the private ownership of marine resources.

In many of the places where ITQs have been introduced they have begun to provide neat solutions to complex conflicts, such as native claims to fisheries. ITQs have also reduced the costs of fisheries management by reducing subsidies and reducing fishing capacity. In Alaska, IFQs (Individual Fishing Quotas – a form of ITQs) have eliminated the infamous and dangerous race for fish known as the halibut derby. The fishery there is now less dangerous, there are fewer boats, and fresh, quality halibut is available for many more than two weeks a year. Additionally, a number of deckhands have started to invest in these ITQs to ensure their employment and to steady their income (Lundsten, 1997).

By reducing uncertainty about future harvests, ITQ owners have been able to capitalise on the expected future returns of

---

[7] Describing a 1993 decision by the hoki fleet not to fish an extra 50,000 tons of fish allocated to them by the government.

their quota. They are also much more inclined to face trade-offs and opportunity costs, and to benefit from having something to retire on. Even some banks are beginning to accept licences as collateral, improving access to the fishery by making loans easier to secure. In Iceland, ITQs cannot legally be used as collateral, but banks have worked out arrangements whereby the fishing vessel is the collateral, and vessel owners contract with the bank not to sell any ITQ without first consulting the bank (Eythorsson, 1996).

ITQs in New Zealand

ITQs were first widely introduced in New Zealand in 1986, and today, following numerous improvements, the experiment appears to have been tremendously successful. Fish stocks are generally healthy and ITQs seem to be on the verge of evolving into real private property rights. Worlds apart from the EU fisheries and the CFP, the New Zealand fishing industry receives no government subsidies and pays the full cost of all fisheries management services (see McClurg, 1997, and Sharp, 1997).

Until the introduction of ITQs, fisheries management in New Zealand followed a familiar pattern. Since 1960 the government had not only condoned free entry into the fisheries but subsidised their development. This produced the predictable result: falling fish stocks coupled with rising investment in fishing capital (Clark *et al.*, 1988). In the late 1970s the government responded by limiting entry in some fisheries, but fishing pressure continued to increase as those already in the fisheries simply increased their efforts.

The deplorable state of many inshore fisheries led to the Fisheries Act of 1983, which consolidated all previous legislation and, most importantly, set out both to improve resource conservation and to increase economic returns from the fisheries (Arnason, 1997). This led to the creation of tradable quotas for some of the deep-water fisheries and, in October 1986, 10-year ITQs were introduced for all significant commercial finfish species with the creation of the Quota Management System (QMS).

The initial attempt at ITQs had many drawbacks. First, quotas were issued on the basis of tonnage, and so the Fisheries Ministry

41

was forced to buy back quota whenever the total catch was lowered. Second, a generous appeals process was created to address any perceived inequities in the allocation process. Out of the 1,800 quotas determined initially, 1,400 objections were lodged. After these were settled, there was an additional opportunity to lodge a complaint with the Quota Appeal Authority, and 1,100 quota holders responded. Eventually these disputes were finally laid to rest. In 1990 the system changed and ITQs became a right to a per centage of the total allowable catch, still determined by the government.

The next step came in 1992 when the government was finally able to settle the issue of native fishing claims, a source of great uncertainty for some time (McClurg, 1997). Under the 1840 Treaty of Waitangi between the native Maori and the European settlers, the Maori were guaranteed the 'full, exclusive and undisturbed possession of their fisheries'. The advent of ITQs provided an opportunity for the Maori to mount a stronger legal challenge against the crown. The government eventually settled these claims by granting the Maori ITQs and a 50 per cent share of a large fishing company (Sealord Products Ltd.).

Other problems were caused by uncertainty as to the security of ITQs and threats by the government heavily to tax the quotas. The government wanted to capture all of the value created by an ITQ (called the resource rent), and for a while government policy was to increase taxes gradually until the value of the annual traded quota approached zero (Hide and Ackroyd, 1990). Destruction of the value of the quota in this way would have eliminated any incentive to steward the resource, which was the whole point of creating the ITQ system in the first place. Fortunately, in 1994 the taxes on resource rents were scrapped and ITQs were changed to perpetual rights.

These improvements have moved ITQs incrementally closer to formal private property rights (McClurg, 1997). Even without the legal right to manage or enhance their fisheries, quota owners have started to organise self-regulating management companies. These management companies impose sanctions on non-complying shareholders and collect funds to help enforce restricted harvests, spread catches over time, redefine management areas and co-ordinate research and enhancement projects. Government still demands cost recovery fees for management services, but these are decreasing as many quota owner companies purchase management science themselves. In many cases the Ministry of Fisheries simply rubber stamps industry-funded scientific recommendations.

The effects of the ITQ system can be seen clearly in two fisheries. Overfishing before the advent of ITQs decimated New Zealand paua (abalone). After ITQs were created, quota owners in the Chatham Islands stopped competing with one another and instead co-operated to limit harvests and invest in research, forming the Chatham Islands' Shellfish Reseeding Association 'to foster and promote the enhancement of the fishery stock in the Chatham Islands'. (Hide and Ackroyd, 1990, p. 43) These ITQs have also evolved to represent exclusive rights to certain areas instead of harvests, and paua management companies are rapidly forming.

Perhaps the best-known catch from New Zealand is orange roughy (89 per cent of which is exported to the United States) (New Zealand Fishing Industry Board, 1997). These deep-water fish live at depths of 750 to 1,200 metres and recent reports have found that they commonly live to be over 100 years old. In 1991 all of the orange roughy quota holders formed the Exploratory Fishing Company (ORH 3B) Limited, which binds them to strict commercial contract and funds both management science and research, including research cruises to look for new fishing grounds (Stevens, 1993). The slow growth of the orange roughy has lately led environmentalists to decry their over-exploitation. Some stocks were depleted on the advice of government science, but since the industry took the lead with the formation of the ORH 3B company, orange roughy has been fished far more conservatively.

Problems with ITQs

Most of the problems created by ITQs arise because they are not real private property rights. ITQs simply confer an access right to a per centage of an annual harvest determined by fisheries regulators. Thus, ITQs should *not* be confused with any sort of private property rights to the fish themselves. ITQs do seem to be evolving ever closer to private property rights in New

Zealand, but this is certainly not the case everywhere.

In fact, in many cases, ITQs are explicitly created so that they cannot evolve into any sort of stronger right. The IFQ programme in Alaska, for example, specifically states that the IFQs are not private property rights and can be taken without compensation at any time.

Subjecting ITQs to bureaucratic whim severely limits the positive incentives that ITQs are created to mimic. In these cases they remain publicly managed and susceptible to many of the pitfalls discussed earlier, limiting the impetus for innovation and resource enhancement, and discouraging the exploration of alternative resource uses. For example, in some cases it may be more efficient to own the rights to a particular area rather than the rights to particular species (see Chapter 4).

Thus, careful consideration is crucial before ITQs are implemented. In particular, the central lesson from the New Zealand experience should always be borne in mind: the closer an ITQ resembles a private property right, the greater the chance for success. The closer it comes to government management, the less effective it becomes.

In addition, the less ITQs approximate private rights, the more they have the potential to become government-enforced privileges, much like taxi cab medallions in New York City. (The number of these medallions is fixed and so their owners have a vested interest in maintaining the *status quo*.) Such ITQs might limit competition and stifle innovation, the exact opposite of what they were set up to accomplish. Substituting fish species and opportunities to benefit from improving the fishery reduce the chances that this will happen, but as government involvement in the management of ITQs increases, so does the potential for ITQs to become 'medallions'.

Some fish processors in the US today closely resemble medallion owners. They have invested heavily in the current system, which supplies huge amounts of fish in very short bursts. For example, some processors maintain large inventories of frozen fish which would, under an ITQ system, be inventoried in the ocean. These processors naturally resist any changes that make their capital investments redundant.

There is also a real danger that ITQs will be used to tax the fishing industry, which would reduce the positive incentives created by ITQs to conserve resources, innovate new techniques, invest in research and enhance the fishery. Taxing away the value of an ITQ would also have a negative impact on cost-reducing activities, encourage government to meddle in the fisheries to try to increase tax revenue, create perverse incentives for industry to lower total catches, and impede collective action to try to raise the value of the quota (Johnson, 1993). Such was the case in New Zealand before the idea of capturing resource rents was finally abandoned, and it appears to be a growing issue in Iceland (Gissurarson, forthcoming).

The real dangers that ITQs present all lie in failing to divorce politics from conservation. Creating ITQs addresses open access problems, but rigidly and inappropriately defined ITQs will not be much of an improvement over the *status quo*. Until fishing rights are safeguarded from the vagaries of government control, the incentive to harvest stocks sustainably will remain weak.

Opposition to ITQs

For many who favour a private property rights approach to conservation, ITQs do not go nearly far enough. Much of the opposition to ITQs, however, stems from an opposition to any sort of privatisation whatsoever.

Some of this opposition makes perfect sense. Any programme that creates ITQs will necessarily involve a political allocation. Because private institutions have not been given the chance to evolve, there are many more stakeholders in the fishery than there would be otherwise. Some will expect to come out ahead whilst others will expect to be worse off under the new system, and the latter will be likely to oppose any changes vehemently. ITQs are often distributed on the basis of historical catch, which sounds reasonable but still rankles with many. Many fishers are savvy, and they know that the most important indicator of distribution is political clout – if they do not have it, they will not trust any change in the current system.

Other arguments against ITQs frequently stem either from those who are benefiting under the current system (such as successful rent-seekers) or from those who simply believe that state control still works best. However, given the success of ITQ programmes elsewhere and the tenuous claim that state control is optimal, this opposition usually takes the form of other fears, which in many cases are unfounded.

One of the most common of these fears is consolidation. Some claim that the quota system in New Zealand has excluded 'small-scale and independent fishers from fisheries, which fall increasingly under the control of large, profit seeking corporations' (Duncan, 1996, p. 104), but this is far from the case. Consolidation in New Zealand has occurred, but primarily in the offshore fisheries for orange roughy, hoki and squid that have always involved large, capital-intensive efforts. The number of vessels in the full-time, smaller-scale domestic fleet, however, has remained relatively constant over the past decade (McClurg, 1997). If it is accepted that there are too many boats chasing too few fish (and it generally is), then some reduction of the fleet can only be expected. At least when everyone receives an initial quota, they only leave the fishery by choice. (Consolidation may, however, become more likely if rights are auctioned rather than allocated on the basis of historical involvement in the fisheries.)

Fears of reductions in employment also seem to be unfounded. While in some cases there will probably be fewer jobs on the water, with the end of fishing derbies, far more fresh, quality fish will reach the docks, increasing opportunities in fish processing. ITQs have improved the opportunities for steady employment in Alaska (Lundsten, 1997), and in Atlantic Canada, some inshore fishing operations have kept the same number of employees through the transition to ITQs by investing in more processing (d'Entremont, 1996).

Another concern raised over the implementation of ITQs is the effect that they will have on a fishing community. In some cases this is a specious concern – certainly those communities should be able to decide how they would like to live – but in other cases it stems from the community itself. As mentioned earlier, a homogeneous fishing fleet is much easier to monitor and control, and fears related to out-transfers from the group are certainly reasonable. However, this is not a reason to reject ITQs. In Alaska some Native American communities receive community quotas (called CDQs – community development quotas) and there is no reason to believe that communities that valued

46

cohesiveness could not organise themselves or manage their rights as common rights instead of individual ones.

Few focus their opposition to ITQs on the resource, but one such negative effect may be the practice of highgrading (see Copes, 1986). Highgrading occurs when fishers throw back targeted fish (to their likely deaths) in the hopes of catching larger, more valuable specimens. The practice, which is clearly not good for conservation, is common in non-transferable quota systems that simply limit catches, but is less common in ITQ systems because they encourage increased monitoring and enforcement among quota owners, who benefit from reducing the incidence of the practice. In addition, highgrading is also limited by peer pressure, pride, and the fact that most crews work for a share of the catch – so if they discard some of what they catch then they are earning less for their work.[8] Thus, although highgrading may be a problem, it is unlikely to be a greater problem under ITQs, and when considering the extent of the problem, it is always worth asking, 'Compared to what?' Compared to the *status quo*, ITQs are generally a significant improvement.

---

[8] Personal communication with Evan Walters, a Canadian commercial fisherman, November 1996.

4. Homesteading the Oceans

'The only true limits [to private ownership in the oceans] are ... technology and human ingenuity.' *Kent Jeffreys (1991, p. 23)*

'We herd cows. Why not fish?' *David Barret, hydrodynamic researcher at MIT (quoted in Crittenden, 1991)*

As described earlier, the rapidly changing landscape of the American West at the turn of the century illustrates how private ownership encourages the development of innovative technologies and superior approaches to resource management. Advances in technology such as barbed wire improve resource management by internalising costs and benefits, usually either by 'branding' or 'fencing' resources and making it easier to define, enforce and transfer private property rights.

On land, under the proper institutional framework, technological innovations tend to increase productivity. This chapter discusses the possibility that similar innovations could have the same effect in the oceans. Unfortunately, the relationship between institutions and incentives is often poorly understood, so technology is blamed for causing problems when the real culprit is inappropriate institutions. For example, advanced technologies that allow fishing boats to 'vacuum the seas' are a rational response to the incentives faced by fishers under a government-managed system that encourages them to introduce technological advances into the adversarial relationship between the regulators and the regulated.

To make matters worse, not only have private institutions and technology not been allowed to evolve together, they have frequently been actively encouraged to diverge. Governments often subsidise technological investments to help fishers keep up with the restrictions imposed on them to stem the depletion that was caused by government policies in the first place. Under the Common Fisheries Policy these funds are earmarked for 'modernisation'.

In some cases severe restrictions on technology may stem overcapitalisation, but this rarely benefits the fishery. Once again oysters provide a good example of the effects of two different régimes. Oyster harvests on the depleted public beds in Maryland are restricted in various ways, including the kinds of technologies that can be used to harvest oysters.[9] Contrast this with the situation in Washington state where there is clear title to the tidelands: oysters are not only harvested by relatively modern means, but harvests have soared over the years on beds enhanced with seed from the Washington oyster growers' own high-tech hatcheries.

Just as the Washington oyster growers staked their claims to the tidelands in the 19th century, the potential exists today to 'homestead' the oceans. In fact, many technologies already exist that could be used to define and protect private property in the oceans, just as branding and barbed wire did in the frontier American West. Moreover, the rate of innovation would accelerate if encouraged by private property institutions. The following are just a few examples of the host of existing technologies which could be applied to 'branding' and 'fencing' marine species (see M. De Alessi, 1997b).

Branding Technologies

In British Columbia a firm called Elemental Research can identify the exact origin of individual salmon by analysing its fish scales. Each and every stream has a unique chemical signature, and Elemental Research identifies the stream a fish has come from using a non-lethal technique involving lasers and mass spectrometry, thereby accurately identifying even the smallest individual populations of salmon.

In a similar way a bone in a fish's inner ear, called an otolith, can be used to identify particular populations of fish (Kingsmill, 1993). Otoliths, which aid in balance, grow in concentric layers, producing daily rings much like those produced annually on a tree. These rings are unique and depend on the surrounding environmental conditions. For fish raised in a hatchery, distinct

---

[9] Restrictions in other Maryland fisheries are also severe; for example, the skipjack fleet is the last commercial fishing fleet in the US still powered by sail.

patterns can be made in fish otoliths simply by altering water temperatures. So far this technique has limited applications because there is no way to examine live fish.

Genetic research provides much of the same information as otolith research. A process known as electrophoresis, also described as genetic fingerprinting, can be used to determine the origins of anadromous fish and, in some cases, even the very stream that the fish hatched in (*Pacific Fishing*, 1989).

In 1993, scientists at Cornell used the Integrated Undersea Surveillance System (IUSS) to track a single blue whale for nearly 43 days without the use of tags or radio beacons. The song-like sounds of whales are as distinct as human voices, so that individual whales can be identified in almost the same way that voice prints identify people. The IUSS, a military technology left over from the Cold War, is a cohesive network of fixed and mobile acoustic devices for monitoring the oceans. It takes advantage of the different layers of temperature and salinity in most of the world's oceans that trap certain acoustic waves, such as those from submarines, underwater earthquakes, or cetaceans (the group of mammals that includes whales) and allows them to be detected from afar (Nishimura, 1994).

Large animals can also be tracked using satellites. Transmitters have been attached to manatees that use satellite telemetry to communicate the exact location, identity, water temperature and direction in which a manatee appears to be headed (O'Shea, 1994).

Fencing Technologies

In addition to providing a means of monitoring individual 'branded' animals, satellites can also be used to monitor the location of fishers and thereby enable monitors to know when a 'fence' has been broached.

Heat-sensitive satellites monitoring a particular area are able not only to keep track of a ship's location, but also its activity. Using Advanced Very High Resolution Radiometry (AVHRR) and Synthetic Aperture Radar (SAR), scientists at Natural Resources Consultants in Seattle and the Pacific Remote Sensing Alliance in Spokane, Washington, can tell whether ships are towing nets or not (Freberg *et al.*, 1992). When a ship tows a net, its engines work harder and this is reflected in the heat profile of the ship, which is detected by the satellites.

Devices exist that can be placed on board a fishing vessel either constantly to relay its exact location to a monitor via satellite or periodically to record the information in a 'black box'. This technology is currently used in New Zealand and has been proposed for use by the EU as well, but because it would be expensive to force onto the fishing industry, there has been much resistance. In March 1997 EU fisheries ministers agreed on a regulation to set up a satellite monitoring system for fishing vessels above 20 metres in length which will begin to enter into force, gradually, in June 1998. Forcing ships to carry these devices is an expensive measure (i.e. more 'modernisation' funds) that would likely be taken up by the fishers themselves if a private arrangement existed.

Satellite technologies also provide fishers with information concerning the likely whereabouts of schools of fish. A firm called Ocean Imaging developed one such technology, which relays maps of up-to-the-minute heat profiles of the ocean's surface to fishing vessels at sea (Silvern, 1992). Commercial fishers and sport fishing charter boat captains pay a premium for this service because the interface between warm and cool waters provides accurate clues to the whereabouts of certain species of fish. Smaller fish like the cool, nutrient-rich waters, but the visibility is better in the warmer nutrient-poor water. Predators like marlin that depend on their eyesight to hunt are commonly found at the interface, hoping the smaller fish will stray into warm water.

Electronic tags that record depth and water temperature are beginning to shed light on the migrations of groundfish in the North Sea. Species like plaice and cod use tidal streams to migrate, both in their daily feeding patterns and in longer spawning migrations. Using these tags, researchers have been able to reconstruct the tracks of plaice migrating between the southern North Sea and their spawning grounds in the eastern English Channel or Northeast coast of England (Metcalfe and Arnold, 1997).

Researchers in France are currently working on ways to use sound to fence in fish (*Fish Farming International*, 1996). This experimental, 'cageless' method will keep fish in a particular area by using a system of sonar buoys to generate sounds that the fish have been conditioned to associate with the distribution of food.

Scientists at MIT are working on a 'robo-tuna' that mimics the very efficient propulsion system of real tuna (Crittenden, 1994). If successful this autonomous underwater vehicle (AUV), or others like it, might stay at sea for up to six months patrolling spawning grounds or remote shellfish beds. Using two-way networks similar to those used for cellular telephones, these AUVs will be able to receive instructions and send data back to land via surface buoys and satellite relays (Fricke, 1994). They may even be able to act as fish-herders, goading schools of fish from feeding ground to feeding ground and notifying the owners about any unauthorised fishing. Or it might be cost-effective to use them to monitor single species such as whales and Giant Bluefin Tuna - which routinely fetch up to $30,000 at the Tokyo seafood market (Seabrook, 1994).

Technologies Enable Private Ownership

These technologies demonstrate the vast potential for private ownership to evolve in the oceans if given the chance. So far they have evolved without the impetus to apply them to protecting and monitoring private property. But if those incentives existed, no doubt the rate of innovation would skyrocket. In order to see why this would be the case, compare once again the world's oceans with the frontier American West, where barbed wire was developed not by ranchers, but by manufacturers of wire in search of new markets. Satellite monitoring in the Pacific Northwest is developing for exactly the same reason. As the struggle over black boxes by the EU demonstrates, selling a committee on a new idea is inherently more difficult that selling it to an individual – if that individual can gain from the innovation. Private property systems are much more favourable to technological and institutional change.

It is also worth noting that, as impressive as technological innovations can be, institutions matter most. Advanced technologies are far from crucial for private management to succeed. Just because something is technologically feasible does not mean that it will be optimal.

Consider the plight of certain elephant populations in Africa. In most areas where elephants may not be owned privately they have declined dramatically (see Sugg and Kreuter, 1995). There is no doubt that it is theoretically possible to put a satellite transmitter on each and every elephant and to monitor them day and night to prevent poaching. But even the most rabid animal rights activists do not propose this, presumably because the costs would be astronomical, and, at the very least, it would also imply ownership and/or domestication. By the same token, no one in his or her right mind would argue that by allowing poverty-stricken rural communities to own elephants they would immediately invest in satellite monitoring systems. Nevertheless, turning control over elephants to local populations is the best way to ensure their effective conservation, as the experience of Zimbabwe, Namibia and South Africa attests. It radically changes the motivations of the people whose lives are most affected by these massive and potentially dangerous creatures. When villagers see that they can benefit from conserving the elephants that roam their land, they protect them instead of poaching them or destroying their habitat.

By extension, technological improvements are important but not crucial to improved marine resource management: the tools are important, but institutions matter the most.

Aquaculture

'A decade ago, a fish Malthusian might have predicted the end of salmon as a food. Human ingenuity seems to have beaten nature once again.' *(Fleming Meeks, 1990)*

While the world fish catch has stagnated in recent years, aquaculture production has grown dramatically. It is now responsible for nearly 20 per cent of the world fish production, and is one of the world's fastest growing industries. In 1991, world aquaculture production was approximately 13 million metric tons, double what it was seven years before (FAO, 1993b). By 1995 that number had jumped to over 21 million metric tons (FAO, 1997).

By now, the reason for these increases should be obvious. Of course, some aquaculture operations have been heavily subsidised, but the most important reason for aquaculture's success has been that there is no tragedy of the commons within an aquaculture facility. A fish not harvested today will be there tomorrow, normal rates of mortality notwithstanding. Private ownership has invigorated entrepreneurs to tinker, to experiment, and to innovate. Salmon is one of the most commonly farmed species, and fish farmers have developed ways to manage their fish in remarkable ways. Through genetic manipulations as well as environmental and dietary control, aquaculturalists increase the fat content for sushi chefs and reduce it for producers of smoked salmon. They can also increase a salmon's nutritional value, adjust its brilliant orange colour, or set the flavour to bold or mild (Bittman, 1996).

One great advantage of aquaculture is the stability of supply. Farm-raised fish are often brought to market within a day of being harvested, while wild-caught fish sometimes take a week. Aquaculture facilities have fresh fish in holding tanks and can either slow or accelerate growth as they please. Markets and restaurants can count year round on the availability of fresh fish of uniform quality and size. No wild fishery approaches that.

Another reason for the success of aquaculture is the survival rate of juveniles; only 10 per cent of salmon fry survive in the wild whereas in captivity the number jumps to almost 90 per cent (Munk, 1995). In 1980, the total world-wide catch of salmon (wild and farmed) was just over 10,000 metric tons (Meeks, 1990). In 1990, farmed salmon alone from Norway, Chile, Scotland, Canada, and Iceland amounted to over 220,000 metric tons. As a result, in real terms, the retail price of salmon in 1990 was about half of what it was in 1980 (Meeks, 1990). Shrimp aquaculture is booming as well, and the production of farmed shrimp should exceed the wild harvest by the year 2000 (Gujja and Finger-Stich, 1996).

Besides salmon and shrimp, catfish and tilapia are common aquaculture species. The majority of fish grown around the world is finfish (approximately 70 per cent), followed by molluscs such as oysters and clams (24 per cent); crustaceans, mostly shrimp (6 per cent), make up the rest (FAO, 1993b).

Aquaculture is not without its problems. Most aquaculture

(approximately two-thirds) occurs near the coast or in shallow estuaries where pollution from outside sources can cripple an aquaculture operation. In addition, intensive aquaculture in these areas can produce significant amounts of organic pollution, which can lead to reduced levels of oxygen in the water and an increase in quick-growing algae that is harmful to marine life. In some cases there is also growing concern over the antibiotics used. Private solutions to pollution are discussed in the next section, but it is worth noting that when pollution does occur, it is generally because property rights have not been appropriately defined and/or are not readily enforceable. Government subsidies and incentives to expropriate coastal areas for aquaculture often further undermine nearshore private property rights.

Many environmentalists ignore these perverse incentives and instead simply vilify aquaculture in developing nations, particularly Thailand and Ecuador, holding it singly responsible for vast amounts of coastal habitat destruction. They compare shrimp farming to slash-and-burn agriculture and have even gone so far as to hold mock trials for poor Thai shrimp farmers in New York, accusing them of 'despoiling their country's coastal wetlands by raising shrimp'. (Mydans, 1996) In one sense they are right. According to United Nations estimates, in Thailand only 40,000 acres of mangrove forest remain, down from nearly a million acres just 30 years ago (Mydans, 1996). Shrimp farming has certainly been a significant factor in this decline. Indeed, abandoned ponds can 'saturate the surrounding soil with salt and pollute the land and water with a chemical sludge made up of fertiliser and antibiotics as well as larvicides, shrimp feed and waste'. (Mydans, 1996). But the root cause of this problem is a lack of secure property rights in marine resources, which is the result of government intervention, *not* an inherent feature of aquaculturists (who are merely operating within the incentive structure defined by the extant institutions).

In Thailand, aquaculture is heavily subsidised and in many cases farms are built in areas that were previously managed much more sustainably by a system of customary tenure (C. Bailey, 1988). In Malaysia, the Land Acquisition Act was amended in 1991 to allow the state to grab land for any reason deemed beneficial to economic development, including the construction of fish ponds (Murray, 1995). Similarly in Ecuador, bribes, corrupt government partnerships and land grabs are common because 'by law, coastal beaches, salt water marshes, and everything else below the high tide line is a national patrimony'. (Southgate, 1992). Not only shrimp farms but city slums regularly invade these areas, even in national ecological preserves (Southgate, 1992).

Alfredo Quarto, a director of the Mangrove Action Project, has pointed out that the main reason why shrimp farmers choose to clear mangrove forests is that they are usually government owned (Weber, 1996). In other words, government sanctioned open access and expropriation of common property rights are what is really to blame for coastal habitat destruction in places like Thailand.

Nearshore aquaculture problems can often be solved by moving operations offshore, where water circulation is better and risks from pollution, both exogenous and endogenous, are limited. Offshore aquaculture is now beginning to move beyond the experimental stage. The engineering problems of raising fish far from protected shores are substantial. Nevertheless, offshore net pens and cages are increasingly appearing off the coasts of places like Norway and Ireland.

One of the greatest setbacks for offshore aquaculture is the question of tenure. For this reason one of the more promising avenues involves utilising decommissioned oil rigs. These rigs offer a fixed platform over ground that has already been leased for oil exploration. Most oil leases specify that they are only for oil production, which complicates the matter, but using existing structures is still promising – they would certainly be far cheaper than starting from scratch.

Self-contained, indoor aquaculture facilities are another relatively new development, but one with tremendous potential. Aquafuture, a firm in Massachusetts, has already had some success raising striped bass in a closed tank system (Herring, 1994). The process uses much less water and feed than conventional fish farms, produces fewer wastes that are easily converted to fertiliser, and by changing the water temperature fish can be grown to market size either faster or slower than in the wild depending on the current market. The enclosed environment is also more sanitary, so Aquafuture's mortality rate is half the industry average.

5. The Environmental Benefits of Owning the Oceans

'Dropping one of these rigs [to create an artificial reef] in the middle of this vast expanse of mud bottom is like putting an oasis in the desert.' Hal Osburn, Texas Parks and Wildlife (quoted on CNN's Future Watch, 1993)

The extension of private ownership into the marine environment would not only transform the state of the world's fisheries, it would vastly improve marine conservation in general. In fact, it has already demonstrated its potential for increasing and protecting habitat, reducing bycatch (see p. 62), fighting pollution, resolving the differences between commercial and recreational fishing and protecting endangered species.

Habitat Enhancement

Artificial reefs offer a singular opportunity to enhance the marine environment. By increasing the surface area available for small encrusting organisms to latch onto or by creating refuges for larger animals, sunken structures both create and enhance marine habitat. They frequently increase fish and other living populations in a given area by providing habitat for creatures that otherwise would not have a place to settle. On the other hand, they may also simply attract fish to a particular area, concentrating them but not producing them.

Of course, every artificial reef is different, and how much marine life is produced versus how much is attracted (possibly even taken away from other sites), varies substantially from reef to reef and is very difficult to measure (see Lindberg, 1997). A system of private ownership over artificial reefs would, however, no doubt concentrate efforts on fabricating reefs that had a positive impact on production.

Fishing communities have known about artificial reefs for centuries, but without secure tenure few reefs are created privately today. That is unfortunate because artificial reefs provide excellent opportunities not only for fishing, but also for

58

scuba diving, scientific research, as a nursery for commercial fisheries, and even simply for enhancing biodiversity for its own sake. Just as millions of homeowners create lovely private gardens in their backyards, so too could artificial reef owners.

Some of this creativity is evident in Japan, where artificial reefs are owned by the fishing co-operatives. These co-operatives actively create artificial reefs, protect them from development and pollution and work diligently to improve artificial reef technology (National Research Council, 1994). In fact, artificial reef technology in Japan is years ahead of the rest of the world.[10]

In the US, concrete moulds and junked cars are the cutting edge of artificial reef technology. In Japan, reefs are manufactured from all manner of items for all manner of purposes, from 'futon cages' that hold groups of rocks together, to reefs specifically designed for abalone and sea urchins, to plastic fronds that attract species normally found on kelp.

Around the rest of the world, artificial reefs are created opportunistically, so the most common building blocks are waste materials. One of the most effective pieces of junk used to form artificial reefs is decommissioned oil rigs. Studies have shown that the steel in most rigs will last up to 300 years underwater (Sayre, 1995).

Offshore oil exploration began in earnest in the 1960s, and since then thousands of offshore oil rigs have been built around the world. The productive lives of many of the older structures are coming to an end, and many will be decommissioned in the near future. Turning rigs into reefs has been very popular in the Gulf of Mexico where, since 1985, over 100 platforms belonging to 36 different oil companies (about 10 per cent of the rigs decommissioned in the Gulf) have been turned into reefs, primarily off the Texas and Louisiana coast (Corzine, 1995). Oil companies split the cost savings of removal with the states (a very lucrative proposition), the states assume all liability for them and the reefs then become public property. Thus there is a strong incentive to create the reefs, but little or no reason to look

---

[10] The reef-building enterprises of these co-operatives, as mentioned earlier, are heavily subsidised, but this does not change the fact that private ownership is what motivates their investment in habitat enhancement and protection.

after them once they are sunk.

The first oil rigs in the North Sea appeared in 1967 and now number over 400. Of these, over 200 are owned by UK companies. According to the UK Offshore Operators Association, in the next 10 years 50 will have to be decommissioned at a cost of approximately $2.25 billion. (Pearce, 1995). What to do with these rigs is serious business.

Tensions erupted over the question of rig disposal in the North Sea in 1995 when members of Greenpeace occupied the Brent Spar, an obsolete oil storage tank due to be sunk. The Greenpeace campaign was tremendously successful, eliciting the sympathy of the media and the governments of Germany and the Netherlands. One activist even firebombed a Shell gas station in Germany. The outcry over the proposed sinking of the Brent Spar arose in part because of the supposed levels of radioactivity and heavy metals in the structure, but Martin Angel of the Institute of Oceanographic Studies in Surrey (UK) points out that the radioactivity was not much more than in a typical granite building in Aberdeen, and that hydrothermal vents on the deep ocean floor constantly discharge large amounts of similar heavy metals (Pearce, 1995).

The whole imbroglio stemmed from the same scenario faced by artificial reef creators in the Gulf. There was a tremendous financial incentive to sink the Brent Spar, but none to worry about where it ended up.

The deep, notoriously rough waters of the North Sea form a far different environment from the Gulf of Mexico, yet even without any appeal to sports-fishers or scuba divers, sunken rigs could still be very valuable to commercial fisheries. In places like Grimsby in the UK local fishers frequently dump old cars into the waters to create a haven for fish by keeping out trawlers (Robins, 1995). In fact there was even a town in Scotland that wanted the Brent Spar to be dumped off its shores for just that purpose. Some have also proposed that rigs in the North Sea and the no-fishing zones that surround them have provided a real 'boost to North Sea fish stocks' (Booker, 1997).

These issues could all be resolved, of course, if only the leasing arrangements that exist for offshore oil exploration were extended to include habitat enhancement.

In two other states on the Gulf of Mexico, Alabama and Florida, even a very limited sense of ownership over artificial reefs has resulted in a great deal of private initiative (M. De Alessi, 1997c). These two states have created large areas where private individuals and groups are allowed to create reefs out of certain permitted structures. The reefs are public property as soon as they hit the water, but the vague proprietary ownership that comes from knowing the exact location of a reef has been enough to spur private reef creation. Of course the fleeting nature of this 'ownership' has not encouraged any interest in long-term stewardship, but it does demonstrate that the private response would be significant.

Marine Reserves

Much like artificial reefs, marine reserves offer an opportunity to enhance the marine environment. Just what effect they may have in any given situation, however, is very uncertain (Schmidt, 1997). Nevertheless, there is a growing interest around the world in the creation of marine reserves – biologist Jane Lubchenco recently called for increasing the per centage of the ocean's surface covered by marine reserves from today's one-quarter of one per cent to 20 per cent by the year 2020 (Schmidt, 1997).

Unfortunately, there seems to be little faith that marine reserves could be created privately, but as is the case for artificial reefs and land-based nature reserves,[11] privately created marine reserves would most likely be far more effective than reserves created and enforced by states. In fact, fishers often strongly oppose state-mandated reserves, as was the case in the Florida Keys (Schmidt, 1997).

If reserves are effective, they would most likely occur naturally as a result of private arrangements in the fisheries. In Negros Oriental in the Philippines, marine reserves seem to have demonstrated some success. One observer there has commented that reserves 'are, in effect, natural fish farms' (Fenner, 1997). The success of this reserve underscores the crucial importance of a sense of ownership by the surrounding community of fishers,

---

[11] On this issue, see for example Michael 't Sas-Rolfes (1995) and Ike Sugg and Urs Kreuter (1994).

who are 'its only effective defenders' (Fenner, 1997). Robert Johannes (1981) similarly found that in places where village control of marine tenure was secure, fishers often enforced no-take zones in areas where fish were known to be spawning or otherwise in danger of depletion.

The proponents of world-wide initiatives to increase the number and size of marine reserves would do well to keep in mind the vast potential of private interests to protect and conserve the marine environment. Private ownership initiatives are likely to result in far more effective conservation areas than would state efforts.

Bycatch Reduction

Fish caught inadvertently while targeting other species are known as bycatch.[12] Some of these species are kept, but many more are discarded. Some discards are low-value species that may not have been kept anyway, but valuable species are also often discarded simply to comply with fishing regulations. This discarded catch is estimated to average 27 million tonnes a year, well over one-quarter of the total world fish catch (Alverson *et al.*, 1994). Not surprisingly, environmentalists and many others decry bycatch as wasteful.

Bycatch in and of itself is not 'wasteful'. Fishing methods are imprecise and even the most selective gear hauls in non-target species. However, forcing valuable species to be thrown back into the sea (to their likely deaths) is clearly ridiculous. A 1990 evaluation of the fisheries in the Gulf of Alaska found that between $20 million and $30 million of commercially valuable crab, halibut, and salmon were discarded annually by fishers who were forced to discard non-target species (Alverson *et al.*, 1994).

A system of private property rights would solve the problem. If an unexpected netful of valuable species landed on deck, one phone call could easily arrange a trade for the right to keep those species. One could even imagine a futures and options market arising for rights to species that might be caught inadvertently. Fishers could then hedge their bets and reduce risk with a

---

12 There is some disagreement over the exact definition of the word bycatch. For these purposes it will refer to all of the non-target species caught, kept or discarded.

portfolio of potential bycatch species. In addition, the incentive to avoid bycatch altogether would skyrocket if non-target species were the property of someone else who would have to be compensated for the loss.

Pollution Abatement

One of the most debilitating problems in the marine environment is pollution. It is often used as a rallying cry for government intervention, but a far better solution is to create private ownership arrangements to internalise its effects. The oyster growers who own tidelands in Washington, for example, have been, for almost a century, the staunchest defenders of water quality in that state (see M. De Alessi, 1996).

Garret Hardin (1968, p. 1,245) believed that

'The tragedy of the commons as a food basket is averted by private property, or something like it. But the air and waters surrounding us cannot readily be fenced, and so the tragedy of the commons as a cesspool must be prevented by different means, by coercive laws or taxing devices that make it cheaper for the polluter to treat his pollutants than to discharge them untreated.'

He was wrong. Private owners have the strongest incentives to devise ways to 'fence' air and water (much like they did in the American West) and, once they have, an institution exists for them to prevent pollution – the common law.

When not superseded by statute law, private owners may utilise the common law to prevent pollution (see Brubaker, 1995, and Yandle, 1997). Under the common law, any activity that damages another's property must cease and the damage be compensated. In addition, riparian owners have an undisputed right to clean water, so in the event of pollution upstream, downstream owners can sue for damages.

Such has been the case in England and Wales, where private rights to salmon in rivers are common. As a result, there is a legal recourse when pollution harms these fisheries. Since its formation in the 1950s, the Angler's Cooperative Association (ACA) has prosecuted 'more than fifteen hundred cases of pollution and recovered hundreds of thousands of pounds in damages to enable riparian owners to restore their fisheries'. (Williams, n.d.). These suits were often directed at the same local authorities responsible for enforcing anti-pollution statutes, and the efforts of the ACA demonstrate the potency of the common law and the danger of a reliance on statutory limitations (Bate, 1994).

Tracing pollution at sea is certainly more difficult than it is in a river or stream, but technology may soon change that. Otoliths, the inner-ear fish bones mentioned earlier, not only make a record of where a fish has lived, but what chemical pollutants it has been exposed to. Additionally, some of the same researchers at MIT working on the 'robo-tuna' are also developing a 'robo-lobster', so named for the attempt to mimic the keen chemical-sensing abilities of the real thing, which could be used someday to track down tirelessly sources of chemical emissions. And in Japan, researchers recently succeeded in breeding fish that turn blue under stress, a common symptom of exposure to harmful pollutants (Whymant, 1997).

Unlike regulations and statutes that force owners to accept a politically determined level of pollution, the common law enables the parties involved to internalise the situation by contracting around their differences. Thus the optimal level of pollution may be non-zero, and will likely be different in every case. In some cases both the polluter and the salmon owner may be better off if the polluter is allowed to buy out the salmon owner. Nevertheless, the full costs of any pollution will be taken into account, which is an important deterrent to any potential polluter. There is certainly no way to determine these costs exogenously, accounting for another failure of the regulatory approach.

Recreational and Commercial Fishing

One of the greatest threats to some commercial fisheries is the growing interest in recreational fisheries around the world. In many cases the recreational catch is substantial, and the political clout of recreational fishers even more so. In the United States, the political allocation of fishing privileges is beginning to favour sports fishing more and more frequently. By sheer numbers alone the sport-fishing community is powerful, and recent voter initiatives have helped to increase recreational opportunities at the expense of commercial ones. For example,

64

voters in states such as California, Louisiana and Florida all recently elected to ban gillnets in near-shore waters. Even in New Zealand, where ITQs are closest to private property rights, some owners of lobster quota are worried that recreational harvests would impinge on their total catch allotments (Sykes, 1997).

In Scotland, however, proponents of sport fishing take a markedly different approach. Because the rights to fish for salmon in Scotland's rivers and streams are clearly defined, salmon fishery regulations there make no distinction between commercial and sports fishing – title to any salmon fishery includes both (Williamson, 1993). Consequently, many near-shore net fishing operations have been bought out by local groups of these owners, sometimes to retire them, in other cases simply to reduce the harvest to the maximum benefit of the two types of fisheries.

Robert Williamson (1993), the Inspector of Salmon and Freshwater Fisheries for Scotland, has pointed out that one of the most remarkable features of this fishery in Scotland is that there is 'no obvious control on fishing effort, ... no licensing of fishers or fishing gear and no direct restrictions on the quantity of gear used or on the amount of fish taken. But, despite all that, the salmon stocks have not been fished-out.'

The same ideas have been played out in Iceland, only on a much larger scale. Private ownership of the rights to fish salmon in inland waters are the norm in Iceland, and this has inspired Orri Vigfusson (1996), chairman of the North Atlantic Salmon Fund (NASF), to go farther afield to protect salmon. By buying out almost the entire offshore salmon fisheries of Greenland and the Faroe Islands, NASF ensured that approximately 400,000 additional salmon returned to home waters in Europe and North America between 1992 and 1995. For this reason Vigfusson strongly supports the extension of private rights into the fisheries – so he has an opportunity to buy them out.

Although not as widespread, rights to salmon in rivers and streams also exist in Canada. Philip Lee describes the different approach that these owners take: 'Riparian owners in New Brunswick have taken action to protect their waters when the federal government seemed to be overseeing the extinction of the

Atlantic Salmon.' (Lee, 1996, p. 41).

Some of the fishing clubs that own salmon rights on stretches of river in places like Scotland are among the most exclusive in the world. But contrary to allegations that sport-fishing in the UK is élitist, opportunities abound for all levels of anglers, and thanks to private ownership, anglers in the UK have generally been spared the ignominy of dams, pollution and overfishing common in the United States (Newman, 1996).

Marine Conservation Through Commerce: the Cayman Turtle Farm

When Irving Naylor and Antony Fisher[13] created a green sea turtle farming operation called Mariculture Ltd. in the Cayman Islands in 1968, the motto of the farm was 'Conservation through Commerce'. At the time, green sea turtle populations were declining world-wide due to a combination of open access harvesting and habitat destruction. So a turtle farm seemed an ideal way to combine commerce (profit was to be made from the sea turtle's valuable meat and shell products) and conservation: the farm would take pressure off the wild stocks by providing an alternative supply, whilst wild stocks would be actively supplemented with farm-bred turtles.

The farm began by ranching the turtles – collecting eggs from the wild that would not otherwise have survived (frequently because of where or the way they had been buried in the sand) and then rearing the turtles at the farm. Even though such a prominent voice as Jacques Cousteau proclaimed that 'If the green sea turtle is to survive, it must be farmed', (Smith, 1988, p. 351), opposition to the farm was strong. Many environmentalists objected to the commercialisation of the species, and were successful in placing trade restrictions on *all* green sea turtle products, farmed or not.

Due to this pressure, Mariculture Ltd. went bankrupt in 1975 and was reorganised as the Cayman Turtle Farm. The battle continued but was lost when the turtle was added to the US endangered species act in 1978, which banned turtle products from even passing through the United States, a crucial hub for

[13] The late Sir Antony Fisher founded the Institute of Economic Affairs.

the farm's international trade. The farm was subsequently taken over by the Cayman government and remains little more than a tourist attraction today.

At the time the green sea turtle was placed on the US endangered species list, the wild population in the Caribbean and the Gulf of Mexico was estimated to be about 5,000 strong. The Cayman Turtle Farm population was close to 80,000 (Smith, 1988).

Both incarnations of the farm were privately financed, and it was on the verge of self-sufficiency (producing enough eggs in-house to forgo collecting in the wild) when it was bankrupted by trade restrictions. Scientific research at the farm provided a wealth of information on the breeding habits and life history of the green sea turtle, and even the farm's detractors, who objected to commercialisation, admitted that the farm was 'of real importance to conservation as well as biology' (Fosdick and Fosdick, 1994). This ill-fated venture demonstrated both the vast potential of private initiatives to benefit the marine environment and, unfortunately, the potentially debilitating effects of government intervention.

6. Conclusions and Policy Implications

'In 1200 AD there were already territorial fishing rights in England and a form of territorial salmon rights throughout the world. ... in the 19th century, the legislative process can only be said to have reduced the characteristics of individual fishing rights.' *Anthony Scott (1988b)*

The erosion of individual fishing rights that Anthony Scott identified has had far-reaching consequences. Indeed, it would not be an exaggeration to say that the oceans are in turmoil as a result. 'Fish wars' between nations are breaking out with increasing frequency. In some cases, once-plentiful fish that formed the staple of many diets have all but disappeared. And the world's fishing fleets are grossly inefficient – all too often there are 'too many boats chasing too few fish', while at the same time millions of perfectly edible fish are discarded simply to comply with arcane rules and regulations.

Innovative reforms in countries like New Zealand and a growing appreciation of the role that traditional knowledge and secure tenure have played in marine conservation over the centuries are positive signs that an understanding of the benefits of private arrangements is growing. However, rent-seeking by fishers' organisations and the actions of some environmental groups have hindered many attempts to move away from centralised political control of the oceans. As a result, private ownership is the exception rather than the rule today. But as the reasons for the decline in the world's fisheries become clearer, private management alternatives will necessarily become increasingly attractive.

Privatising the fish themselves is the most effective way to ensure their conservation and protection, but will rarely be a feasible option, at least for the time being. Privatising access to those resources, however, has already proven to be an effective, viable option. Devices such as ITQs and private reefs, for example, allow for exclusive access to marine resources and have demonstrated positive effects on conservation and stewardship.

ITQs are not a panacea, but they are an important recognition of the power of positive incentives for stewardship and conservation. Every fishery is different, and so are the people involved in determining its future. What is acceptable to them is what matters most, and in many cases ITQs may not be considered ideal. Moving in the direction of a private arrangement, however, is crucial to the health of the resource. Even though ITQs rarely approximate private arrangements, they may often be the most feasible step that can be taken in that direction. For that reason alone, they merit serious consideration.

ITQs and private reefs, although far from perfect, seem to be the most promising route at the moment to the eventual creation of some form of private ownership in fisheries. For ITQs, the greatest single obstacle to their creation is the initial distribution, so it is worth considering how this obstacle might be overcome.

Anyone who thinks that he or she will be worse off under a system of ITQs will naturally oppose its creation. Often this opposition is not to the idea of ITQs, but to the distribution process. In the Pacific Northwest of the United States, some of the most vocal opponents of ITQs are the on-shore fish processors. Their moral outrage would quickly disappear, however, if they thought they would get what they see as a reasonable share of the initial distribution of quota.[14]

Opposition to ITQs also stems from the heterogeneity of the groups involved, and in cases where these differences can be reduced, transaction costs are lower and acceptance is more likely (see Brady, 1997). A common cause of reduced heterogeneity is desperation. In Iceland, for example,

'Only when faced with a disaster in the form of a significant fall in income due to fish stock reductions or a drop in the world market price for fish products, have the interest groups been willing to consider changes in the institutional framework of the fisheries' (Arnason, 1993, p. 207).

Similarly, fisheries with smaller numbers of participants are much more likely to accept ITQs. Terry Anderson and Don Leal compared three distinct groups of herring sac roe fishers on the

---

[14] Personal communication with a fish processor at a fishery colloquium in Seattle, WA, October 1995.

West coast of the United States that differed primarily in fleet size (Anderson and Leal, 1993). Each fleet was made up of a heterogeneous group of fishers and suffered from low returns and a bruising race for fish at the opening of the season. Interestingly, the participants in the smallest fishery (9) worked out a quota system on their own, a slightly larger group (42) was able to lobby for, and get, an ITQ system, but a much larger group (375) did not make any progress.

The situation is analogous to how parties agree to extract oil from common pool fields, where reduced heterogeneity has also led to increased co-operation (Libecap and Wiggins, 1985). Without co-operation, individuals race to extract oil, lowering the overall productivity of the field − much like fishing under open access. In some cases extractors have been able to use the state to enforce co-operative agreements, much like the second group of California herring fishers. This process, called unitization, is more effective the less the individual extractors know about the value of their leases, that is, the less heterogeneous they are. Much like more skilled fishers, owners of higher valued leases may benefit from an open-access régime. When the value of the leases is uncertain, the group is more homogeneous and members are more likely to hedge their bets and to avoid the race for oil.

Unitization schemes demonstrate that opportunities for risk-sharing encourage co-operation. With regard to distribution, it may be worth considering assigning ITQs to groups instead of individuals. These groups could then decide how to distribute them internally, possibly choosing a common property régime instead of an individual one. This also addresses the community concerns mentioned earlier. Orange roughy quota holders in New Zealand did something similar when they all became shareholders in the ORH 3B management company.

It is also important to realise what makes ITQs effective − certainty and flexibility. Any chance that politics may enter into the fishery creates uncertainty, devalues ITQs and reduces conservation incentives. This was the case initially in New Zealand, where for many years 'the spectre of too many fishers chasing too few fish [was] removed by the ITQ system only to be replaced by special interest groups fishing politically on land for a share of the resource'. (Hide and Ackroyd, 1990, p. 1) The fisheries in New Zealand did not begin to move towards self-regulation until the allocation process was clearly over and the ITQs made perpetual.

Flexibility is also critical as rights to an area may be more important than rights to a species. In New Zealand, ITQs for paua (abalone) are rapidly evolving into rights to specific areas. In certain areas in Chile there have been successful experiments granting exclusive rights to benthic resources to artisanal fishery co-operatives. As a result, these areas have been vigorously defended and harvests have improved (Castilla, 1994).

Some proponents of ITQs favour them as a tool to maximise social welfare, to increase efficiency or to decrease overcapitalisation. The implications of such a purely teleological view of the role of ITQs depend upon how the terms 'social welfare', 'efficiency' and 'overcapitalisation' are interpreted – which is often very widely. Needless to say, limitations or restrictions placed on an ITQ system that reduce transferability or prevent consolidation will reduce its effectiveness as a solution to a conservation problem and limit its ability to evolve into a more secure system of private property rights. In turn, this will make the rights less valuable and decrease the motivation for conservation. Of course, some restrictions may in fact be quite useful, but if that is the case they are likely to be discovered and agreed upon by the owners of the ITQs themselves.

Many common property régimes have demonstrated the effectiveness of promoting homogeneity within a group, often by restricting behaviour or out-transfers. Every fishery is different, and the institutions that govern a fishery should allow each fishery or community to set its own rules. Exogenously determined restrictions will generally harm a quota owner, whereas endogenously determined ones are likely to benefit them.

ITQs should be value-neutral. It may be necessary to favour a community or a way of life to get beyond the initial distribution problem, but once rights are allocated, they should not favour one owner over the other. If these communities or ways of life are important to the people involved, they can simply choose not to sell out, or to form their own common property association. Even as ITQs in New Zealand have grown ever more secure, this has only been possible by rebutting frequent attempts politically to re-allocate rights and to promote 'regional socialism' (Beattie, 1996).

ITQs should connote a right to the resource, not just a right to harvest from a publicly owned resource. Many common property régimes confer the same privilege – a harvest right only, but with the crucial difference that the group *owns* the resource. Thus associations in Japan have sometimes benefited tremendously from exploring alternative resource uses. This is particularly critical if ITQs are to work towards reducing conflict not only within the fishing community, but outside of it as well.

Conclusions

The crash of so many once-plentiful marine fisheries is a clear indication of institutional failure. But there is hope for the future. Evidence indicates that fish stocks are highly resilient and are likely to recover rapidly if given the chance (Myers *et al.*, 1995). To give them that chance, government should consider turning over the management of fisheries to private interests. As this paper has attempted to demonstrate, private property, owned individually or in common, offers the best hope of creating incentives for conservation, stimulating the production of new technologies, and protecting the marine environment. Although they may stumble occasionally, mistakes by one individual or group will be more than offset by the successes of others. In the end, the environment, the health of the fish stocks, their harvesters and the fish-eating public will be better off.

From satellite technology used to monitor the oceans to artificial reefs that attract and nurture fish populations to fish farming, technologies exist that could facilitate private ownership in the oceans. Indeed, the mere prospect of ownership in the oceans is already fomenting innovative thinking. One such example is Ocean Farming Inc., a firm in Virginia that hopes to take advantage of limitations on productivity in the oceans that have been created by the limited availability of naturally-occurring iron by fertilising huge swathes of the ocean with a patented iron delivery system (Markels, 1995). Founder Michael Markels (1995) is well aware that for this kind of venture to succeed, 'Some kind of [private] property rights need to be created so that those who bear the costs of [enhancing the oceans] can reap the rewards.'

The issue of liability is also crucial. The problems of open access and government control pervade not only the ways in which fish are harvested, but also the quality of the water everywhere. Making those responsible for pollution liable for their actions is potentially one of the greatest attributes of any private ownership régime.

Conflicts over ocean space will continue to grow, and private ownership is the best mechanism thus far invented to avoid the political carnage that would otherwise occur as recreational and commercial fishers, oil companies, SCUBA divers, environmentalists and others all vie for their piece of the pie. To see how this might work, one need only look to the Audubon Society, which routinely opposes oil exploration on public lands and yet, in its Rainey Wildlife Sanctuary in the Louisiana bayou, has leased the rights to extract oil deposits. Once Audubon faced the trade-offs of an owner, it found ways to profit from the oil deposits in Rainey without compromising its environmental concerns (Adler, 1991).

Although traditional environmental groups in both the United States and Europe have generally resisted supporting market measures to improve fisheries management, that is beginning to change. In the United States the Environmental Defense Fund recently strongly supported the creation of ITQs to 'give value to fish in the water [and] create positive economic incentives to conserve fish' (Fujita and Hopkins, 1995). In Europe, the World Wide Fund for Nature has helped to create the Marine Stewardship Council, which will attempt to label and promote sustainably caught fish so that consumers can exert market pressures on the fishing industry (Maitland, 1996).[15] The outlook for real reform has never been brighter.

The FAO recently announced that world fish production in 1996 was 112.3 million metric tons, another substantial increase. Fish farming contributed most of the growth, but not all. The FAO also estimated that number could increase by 20 million tons if underdeveloped resources were exploited and bycatch

---

[15] For an in-depth study on the effectiveness of eco-labels, see Morris, 1997.

reduced. The potential for tremendous gain is there. All that is required to begin tapping it and to begin restoring those resources that have suffered is to unleash the vast potential of private initiatives to conserve, protect and enhance the marine environment.

References

Acheson, J.M. (1987): 'The Lobster Fiefs Revisited', in McCay and Acheson (1987), pp. 37-65.

Adler, J. (1991): 'Balancing Oil Interests and Ecology', *The Detroit News*, 19 July.

Agnello, R.R, and Donnelley, L. (1975): 'Property Rights and Efficiency in the Oyster Industry', *Journal of Law and Economics*, Vol.18, pp. 521-33.

Alverson, D.L., Freberg, M.H., Murawski, S.A. and Pope, J.G. (1994): 'A Global Assessment of Fisheries Bycatch and Discards', *Fisheries Technical Paper No. 339*, Rome: Food and Agriculture Organization of the United Nations.

Anderson, T.L., and Hill, P.J. (1975): 'The Evolution of Property Rights: A Study of the American West', *Journal of Law and Economics,* Vol.12, pp. 163-79.

Anderson, T.L. and Leal, D. (1993): 'Fishing for Property Rights to Fish', in Meiners and Yandle (1993), pp. 161-83.

Anderson, T.L., and Leal, D. (1991): *Free Market Environmentalism*, San Francisco: Pacific Research Institute for Public Policy.

Arnason, R. (1997): 'Property Rights as an Organizational Framework in Fisheries: The Cases of Six Fishing Nations', in Crowley (1997), pp. 99-144.

Arnason, R. (1993): 'The Icelandic Individual Transferable Quota System: A Descriptive Account', *Marine Resource Economics*, Vol. 8, pp. 201-18.

Article 7 of the Common Fisheries Policy.

Associated Press (1996): press release, June 7.

Bailey, C. (1988): 'The Social Consequences of Tropical Shrimp Mariculture Development', *Ocean and Shoreline Management,* No. 11, pp. 31-44.

Bailey, R. (ed.) (1996): *The True State of the Planet*, New York: The Free Press.

Bate, R. (1994): 'Water Pollution Prevention: A Nuisance Approach', *Economic Affairs*, April, pp. 13-14.

Beattie, Roger (1996): 'Politics or property rights', *Seafood New Zealand*, June.

Bell, F.W. (1972): 'Technological Externalities and Common-Property Resources: An Empirical Study of the U.S. Northern Lobster Fishery', *Journal of Political Economy*, 80, pp. 148-58.

Berkes, F. (ed.) (1995): *Common Property Resources: Ecology and Community-Based Sustainable Development*, London: Belhaven Press.

Berkes, F., Feeny, D., McCay, B. and Acheson, J. (1989): 'The Benefits of the Commons', *Nature*, 340, pp. 91-93.

Bittman, M. (1996): 'Today's Fish: Straight from the Farm', *New York Times*, September 18.

Booker, C. (1997): 'Endangered fish find haven among oil rigs', *Sunday Telegraph,* September 7.

Brady, G.L. (1997): 'United States Fishery Management: the Coase Theorem and Individually Transferable Quotas', in Roberts (1997), pp. 47-65.

Brown, D. (1997): 'Ranching will mean cheaper lobster', *The Daily Telegraph*, February 24.

Brubaker, E. (1995): *Property Rights in the Defence of Nature*, Toronto: Earthscan Publications.

Castilla, J.C. (1994): 'The Chilean Small-Scale Benthic Shell fisheries and the Institutionalization of New Management Practices', *Ecology International Bulletin*, 21, pp. 47-63.

Cheung, S.N. (1970): 'The Structure of a Contract and the Theory of a Non-exclusive Resource', *Journal of Law and Economics*, 13(1), pp. 49-70.

Christy, F. (1996): email contribution to *Fishfolk* internet discussion group, December 6.

Christy, F. (1997): email contribution to *Fishfolk* internet discussion group, February 4.

Christy, F. and Scott, A. (1965): *The Common Wealth in Ocean Fisheries*, Baltimore, MD: The Johns Hopkins Press.

Ciriacy-Wnatrup, S.V. and Bishop, R. (1980): 'Common Property as a Concept in Natural Resources Policy', *Natural Resources Journal*, 15, pp. 713-27.

Clark, I.A., Major, P.J., and Mollet, N. (1988): 'Development and Implementation of New Zealand's ITQ Management System', *Marine Resource Economics,* Vol. 5, pp. 325-49.

Clover, C. (1997): 'Britain plunders the seas', *The Daily Telegraph*, May 26.

Copes, P. (1986): 'A Critical Review of the Individual Quota as a Device in Fisheries Management', *Land Economics*, 62(3), pp. 278-91.

CNN Future Watch (1993): 'Oil rigs to reefs', September 11.

Cordell, J. (1989): *A Sea of Small Boats*, Cambridge, MA: Cultural Survival, Inc.

Corzine, R. (1995): 'From rigs to reefs', *Financial Times*, October 20.

Cowen, T. (ed.) (1988): *The Theory of Market Failure*, Fairfax, VA: George Mason University Press.

Crittenden, J. (1994): untitled article, *The Boston Herald*, October 30.

Crowley, B.L. (ed.) (1997): *Taking Ownership: Property Rights and Fishery Management on the Atlantic Coast*, Halifax: Atlantic Institute for Market Studies.

d'Entremont, J.G. (1996): 'Quotas. Responsibility and Fishing: How They Work Together and in Practice', presentation at the conference 'Rising Tide? Rights-Based Fishing on the Atlantic Coast', St. John's, Newfoundland: Atlantic Institute for Market Studies, November 7-8.

De Alessi, L. (1980): 'The Economics of Property Rights: A Review of the Evidence', *Research in Law and Economics*, Vol. 2, pp. 1-47.

De Alessi, M. (1996): 'Oysters and Willapa Bay', Private Conservation Case Study, Washington, DC: The Center for Private Conservation, March.

De Alessi, M. (1997a): 'Holding out for some local heroes', *New Scientist*, March 8, p.46.

De Alessi, M. (1997b): 'Technologies of Sequestering and Monitoring Ocean Property', in Jones and Walker (1997), pp. 125-50.

De Alessi, M. (1997c): 'How Property Rights Can Spur Artificial Reefs', *The Freeman*, February, pp. 77-79.

Demsetz, H. (1967): 'Toward a Theory of Property Rights', *American Economic Review*, Vol. 57, pp. 347-59.

Denman, D.R. (1984): *Markets Under the Sea*, London: IEA Hobart Paperback No. 17.

Drozdiak, W. (1996): 'France's Net Loss', *Washington Post*, March 15.

Duncan, L. (1995): 'Closed Competition: Fish Quotas in New Zealand', *The Ecologist*, March/April-May/June, p. 97.

Economist, The (1994): 'The tragedy of the oceans', March 19, pp. 21-24.

Economist, The (1996): 'Cyanide Sauce', May 11, p. 35.

Edwards, S.F. (1994): 'Ownership of Renewable Ocean Resources', *Marine Resource Economics*, Vol. 9, pp. 253-73.

Eythorsson, E. (1996): 'Theory and practice of ITQs in Iceland. Privatisation of common fishing rights', *Marine Policy*, Vol. 20, No. 3, pp. 269-81.

Fairlie, S. (1995): 'Who is Weeping Crocodile Tears? Britain's Fishing Industry and the EU Common Fisheries Policy', *The Ecologist*, March/April-May/June, pp. 105-14.

Fairlie, S., Hagler, M., and O'Riordian, B. (1995): 'The Politics of Overfishing', *The Ecologist*, March/April, May/June, p.46-73.

FAO (1992): *Aquaculture production 1984-1990*, Rome: Food and Agriculture Organization of the United Nations.

FAO (1993a): *Marine Fisheries and the Law of the Sea: A Decade of Change*, Rome: Food and Agriculture Organization of the United Nations.

FAO (1993b): *Aquaculture production 1985-1991*, Rome: Food and Agriculture Organization of the United Nations.

FAO (1994): *The State of World Fisheries and Aquaculture*, Rome: Food and Agriculture Organization of the United Nations.

FAO (1997): *The State of World Fisheries and Aquaculture*, Rome: Food and Agriculture Organization of the United Nations.

Fenner, D. (1996): 'To coralist: preserves', email contribution to *coral-list* internet discussion group, February 4.

Fish Farming International (1996): 'Sound will pen fish inside a sea ranch', Vol. 23, No. 4, April.

Fosdick, S. and Fosdick, P. (1994): *Last Chance Lost?*, New York: Irvin S. Naylor.

Freberg, M.H., Brown, E.A., and Wrigley, R. (1992): 'Vessel Localization using AVHRR and SAR Technology', presented at Marine Technology Society Annual Meeting, Washington, DC, October 19.

Fricke, R.J. (1994): 'Down to the Sea in Robots', *Technology Review*, October.

Fujita, R. and Hopkins, D. (1995): 'Market theory can help solve overfishing', *The Oregonian*, September 20.

Gissurarson, H. (forthcoming 1998): *North Atlantic Fisheries: Lessons from Iceland*, London: Institute of Economic Affairs.

Goodlad, J. (1995): 'Work for CFP Reform, not Withdrawal', *Fishing News*, March 17.

Gordon, H.S. (1954): 'The Economic Theory of a Common-Property Resource: The Fishery', *Journal of Political Economy*, Vol. 62, pp. 124-42.

Greenpeace (1993); 'Fishing in Troubled Waters', press release found at http://www.greenpeace.org/~comms/fish/part1.html.

Gujja, B. and Finger-Stich, A. (1996): 'Shrimp Aquaculture's Impact in Asia', *Environment*, September, pp. 12-39.

Hagler, M. (1995): 'Deforestation of the Deep', *The Ecologist*, March/April-May/June, pp. 46-73.

Hanna, S. (1990): 'The Eighteenth Century English Commons: A Model for Ocean Management', *Ocean and Shoreline Management*, Vol. 14, pp. 155-72.

Hardin, G. (1968): 'The Tragedy of the Commons', *Science*, Vol. 162, pp. 1,243-48.

Herring, H.B. (1994): '900,000 Striped Bass, and Not a Fishing Pole in Sight', *New York Times*, November 6.

Hide, R. and Ackroyd, P. (1990): 'Depoliticising Fisheries Management: Chatham Islands' Paua (Abalone) as a Case Study', unpublished report, Lincoln University, New Zealand: Centre for Resource Management.

Higgs, R. (1982): 'Legally Induced Technical Regress in the Washington State Salmon Fishery', *Research in Economic History*, Vol.7, p. 55-86.

Holmes, B. (1994): 'Biologists Sort the Lessons of Fisheries Collapse', *Science*, Vol. 264, May 27, pp. 1,252-53.

Hviding, E. (1991): 'Traditional Institutions and Their Role in the Contemporary Coastal Resource Management in the Pacific Islands', *Naga*, October, pp. 3-9.

Jeffreys, K. (1991): 'Who Should Own the Ocean?', Washington, DC: Competitive Enterprise Institute.

Jeffreys, K. (1996): 'Rescuing the Oceans', in R.Bailey (1996), pp. 295-338.

Johannes, R. (1981): *Words of the Lagoon*, Berkeley: University of California Press.

Johannes, R. and Ripen, M. (1996): 'Environmental, economic and social implications of the fishery for live coral reef food fish in Asia and the Western Pacific', SPC Live Reef Fish Information Bulletin, March.

Johnson, R. (1996): 'Implications of Taxing Quota Value in an Individual Transferable Fishery', *Marine Resource Economics*, Vol. 10, pp. 327-40.

Johnson, R.A. and Libecap, G. (1982): 'Contracting Problems and Regulation: The Case of the Fishery', *American Economic Review*, Vol. 72(5), pp. 1,005-22.

Jones, L. and Walker, M. (eds.) (1997): *Fish or Cut Bait!*, Vancouver, BC: The Fraser Institute.

Karagiannakos, A. (1995): *Fisheries Management in the European Union*, Aldershot, UK: Avebury Publishers.

Karpoff, J.M. (1987): 'Suboptimal Controls in Common Resource Management: The Case of the Fishery', *Journal of Political Economy*, 95, pp. 179-94.

Keen, E. (1983): 'Common Property in Fisheries: Is Sole Ownership an Option?', *Marine Policy*, 7, pp. 197-211.

Kingsmill, S. (1993): 'Ear Stones Speak Volumes to Fish Researchers', *Science*, Vol. 260, pp. 1,233-34.

Leal, D.R. (1996): 'Community-run Fisheries: Preventing the Tragedy of the Commons', in Crowley (1996), pp. 183-220.

Lee, P. (1996): *Home Pool: The Fight to Save the Atlantic Salmon*, Fredricton, NB: Goose Lane Editions.

Libecap, G. and Wiggins, S. (1985): 'The Influence of Private Contractual Failure on Regulation: The Case of Oil Field Unitization', *Journal of Political Economy*, 93(4), pp. 690-714.

Lindberg, W.L. (1997): 'Can Science Resolve the Attraction-Production Issue?', *Fisheries*, Vol. 22, No. 4, April, pp. 10-13.

Ludwig, D., Hilborn, R., Walters, C. (1993): 'Uncertainty, Resource Exploitation, and Conservation: Lessons from History', *Science*, Vol. 260, pp. 17-36.

Lundsten, M. (1997): 'Re: ITQs social effects', email contribution to *Fishfolk* internet discussion group, September 29.

Maitland, A. (1996): 'Unilever in fight to save global fisheries', *Financial Times*, February 22.

Markels, M. (1995): 'Fishing for Markets: Regulation and Ocean Farming', *Regulation*, No.3.

McCay, B. and Acheson, J. (eds.) (1987): *The Question of the Commons*, Tucson: University of Arizona Press.

McCloskey, D.N. (1972): 'The Enclosure of Open Fields: Preface to a Study of Its Impact on the Efficiency of English Agriculture in the Eighteenth Century', *Journal of Economic History*, 32, pp. 15 - 35.

McClurg, T. (1997):'Bureaucratic Management versus Private Property: ITQs in New Zealand after Ten Years', in Jones and Walker (1997), pp.91-105.

McKean, M. and Ostrom, E. (1995): 'Common Property Régimes in the Forest: Just a Relic from the Past?', *Unasylva*, 46, No. 180, pp. 3-15.

Meeks, F. (1990): 'Would you like some salmon with your Big Mac?', *Forbes*, December 24.

Meiners, R. and Yandle, B. (eds.) (1993): *Taking the Environment Seriously*, Lanham, MD: Rowman and Littlefield Publishers.

Melhuish, M. (1995): 'U.K. buyout scheme has plenty of problems', *National Fisherman*, June.

Metcalfe, J.D. and Arnold, G.P. (1997): 'Tracking fish with electronic tags', *Nature*, 387, pp. 665-66.

Miller, D. (1989): 'The Evolution of Mexico's Caribbean Spiny Lobster Fishery', in Berkes (1989), pp. 185-98.

Morris, J. (1997): *Green Goods? Consumers, Product Labels and the Environment*, London: Institute of Economic Affairs Environment Unit.

Munk, N. (1995):'Real fish don't eat pellets', *Forbes*, January 30.

Murray, H. (1995): 'Just Compensation', *Far Eastern Economic Review*, March 9, pp. 14-15.

Mydans, S. (1996): 'Thai Shrimp Farmers Facing Ecologists' Fury', *New York Times*, April 28.

Myers, R.A., Barrowman, N.J., Hutchings, J.A, and Rosenberg, A.A. (1995): 'Population Dynamics of Exploited Fish Stocks at Low Population Levels', *Science*, 269, pp. 1,106-08.

National Research Council (1994): 'Restoring and Protecting Marine Habitat: The Role of Engineering and Technology', Washington, D.C.: National Academy Press.

Neild, R. (1995): *The English, the French and the Oyster*, London: Quiller Press.

New Zealand Fishing Industry Board (1997): information from <www.seafood.co.nz> website.

Newman, C. (1996): 'A Passion for Trout', *National Geographic*, April, pp. 64-85.

Nishimura, C.E. (1994): 'Monitoring Whales and Earthquakes by Using SOSUS', *NRL Review*, Washington, D.C.: Naval Research Laboratory.

O'Shea, T. (1994): 'Manatees', *Scientific American*, July.

Ostrom, E. (1990): *Governing the Commons: The Evolution of Institutions for Collective Action*, Cambridge: Cambridge University Press.

Ostrom, E. (1997): 'Private and Common Property Rights', *Encyclopedia of Law and Economics*, forthcoming.

Pacific Fishing (1989): 'Genetic Fingerprints', November.

Pearce, F. (1995): 'What to do with derricks? Oil drilling platforms in the North Sea', *New Scientist*, September.

Pearse, P. (1980): 'Regulation of Fishing Effort: with special reference to Mediterranean trawl fisheries', FAO Fisheries Technical Paper No. 197, FAO, Rome.

Reuters, October 10, 1996.

Roberts, C.J. (1997): *Deep Water: Fisheries Policy for the Future*, Hume Papers on Public Policy, 5(2), Edinburgh: Edinburgh University Press.

Robins, J. (1995): 'How Brent Spar could be used to save fish stocks', *The Scotsman*, October 3.

Sayre, A. (1995): 'Artificial reef program booming in Gulf', AP Worldstream, November 28.

Schmidt, K.F. (1997):'"No-take" Zones Spark Fisheries Debate', *Science*, Vol. 277, July 25, pp. 489-91.

Scott, A. (1955): 'The Fishery: The Objectives of Sole Ownership', *Journal of Political Economy*, 63, pp. 63-124.

Scott, A. (1988a): 'Development of Property in the Fishery', *Marine Resource Economics*, 5, pp. 289-311.

Scott, A. (1988b): 'Market Solutions to Open-access Commercial Fisheries Problems', presentation at A.P.P.A.M. 10th Annual Research Conference, Seattle, WA, October 27-29.

Seabrook, J. (1994): 'Death of a giant: stalking the disappearing Bluefin Tuna', *Harper's Magazine*, June.

Seijo, J. C. (1993): 'Individual Transferable Grounds in a Community Managed Artisinal Fishery', *Marine Policy*, Vol. 8, p. 78-81.

Sharp, B. (1997): 'From regulated access to transferable harvesting rights: policy insights from New Zealand', *Marine Policy*, 21(6), pp. 501-17.

Silvern, D. (1992): 'For company, space data is catch of the day', *San Diego Union-Tribune*, October 10.

Simon, J. (1996): *The Ultimate Resource 2*, Princeton, NJ: Princeton University Press.

Smith, R.J. (1988): 'Private Solutions to Conservation Problems', in Cowan (1988), pp. 341-60.

Southgate, D. (1992): 'Shrimp Mariculture Development in Ecuador: Some Resource Policy Issues', Working Paper No.5 of the Environment and Natural Resources Policy and Training Project, University of Wisconsin, November.

Stevens, P. (1993): 'ORH 3B – A Role Model', *Seafood New Zealand*, August, p. 3.

Sugg, I. and Kreuter, U. (1994): *Elephants and Ivory: Lessons from the Trade Ban*, London: Institute of Economic Affairs Environment Unit.

Sykes, D. (1997): presentation at the Tri-State Rock Lobster Industry Conference in Adelaide, Australia, September 8.

't Sas-Rolfes, M. (1995): *Rhinos: Conservation, Economics and Trade-offs*, London: Institute of Economic Affairs Environment Unit.

Vigfusson, O. (1996): 'Fast Fish and Sober Captains: Lessons from the North Atlantic Salmon Fund Experience', presentation at the conference on Managing a Wasting Resource: Would Quotas Solve the Problems Facing the West Coast Salmon Fishery?, Vancouver, Canada: The Fraser Institute, May.

Weber, M. (1996): 'The Fish Harvesters: Farm-Raising Salmon and Shrimp makes Millionaires, and also Creates Dead Seas', *E Magazine*, November/December.

Whymant, R. (1997): 'Fish get the blues in war on pollution', *The Times* (London), February 10.

Williams, B. (n.d.): 'The A.C.A. and the Common Law', presented to the Anglers' Co-operative Association Water

Protection Officers' Seminar at the National Water Sports Centre, Holme Pierrepont, Nottingham.

Williamson, R. (1993): 'Scottish Salmon Fishing Rights, a Transferable Property: The Consequences for Administration and Regulation', presented at ICREI Colloquium, Paris, January 28.

Yandle, B. (1997a): 'Anti-trust and the Commons: Cooperation or Collusion?', Washington, DC: Center for Private Conservation, June.

Yandle, B (1997b): *Common Sense and Common Law for the Environment*, Lanham, MD: Rowman and Littlefield Publishers, Inc.